More Advance Praise . . .

"This is a fantastic tool for parents, professionals, and anyone else who connects with persons who have challenges with executive function skills. After a thoughtful, easy-to-read introduction on the difficulties experienced by those who struggle with thinking flexibly and self-monitoring their behavior, a series of concrete solutions is presented along with templates so they can be quickly and easily implemented. The ideas in this book are appropriate for learners of any age group and any ability level, including students who do not have diagnosed disabilities but struggle with executive function skills. *FLIPP the Switch* is a book that every parent and professional should have at the ready, like you might keep a cookbook in a kitchen. It reads like a recipe for success! I personally cannot wait to use it."

> – Aileen Zeitz Collucci, MA, CCC, speech-language pathologist, autism and social-communication consultant, and author of *Big Picture Thinking: Using Central Coherence to Support Social Skills*

"The layout and ease of use of this book is fantastic! The specific tools are organized in a manner that allows educators and/or parents to access specific strategies and put them into practice right away. The visual scales are incredibly useful for students to identify and monitor their behavior and identify how they are feeling. This is a great first step to help them identify what strategies they need to implement in the moment based on their self-reporting."

> – Phyllis Perlroth, lead education specialist, High Tech High North County, intern credential program

"As a physician, I am always in search of information on how to reduce the effects of autism from a biochemical perspective. In addition, as the father of two sons on the spectrum, I rely on practical strategies that help them to navigate their daily lives. *FLIPP the Switch* is just that type of practical help. It is straightforward, easy to use and put into action, and it speaks to executive functioning, which is a huge challenge for my sons and most kids on the spectrum. I highly recommend this book to parents and professionals."

> – Dwayne Cox, MD, anesthesiologist, and father of two on the spectrum

"Problems with attention, working memory, and EF of children and youth at home and at school are commonly cited; however, practical advice about how to ease these problems is rare. That's where this book comes in, with honest and evidence-based recommendations for activities to strengthen working memory and executive function and improve focus and behavior. Readers will find clear descriptions of problems they will recognize – including self-regulation, impulse control, and difficulty linking behavior to its effects – and specific activities they can implement to help individuals with EF difficulties to cope and improve. In *Flipp the Switch,* long-term professional practice interfaces with a solid research base to create a set of strategies that enable parents and practitioners to feel renewed competence in supporting individuals with EF deficits. I predict this book will spend very little time sitting on a shelf."

> -- Rollanda E. O'Connor, PhD, professor and Eady/Hendrick chair in Learning Disabilities, University of California, Riverside, and author of *Teaching Word Recognition, The Handbook of Reading Interventions,* and *Ladders to Literacy*

FLIPP THE SWITCH
Strengthen Executive Function Skills

Sheri Wilkins, PhD, and Carol Burmeister, MA

AAPC PUBLISHING

P.O. Box 23173
Shawnee Mission, Kansas 66283-0173
www.aapcpublishing.net

©2015 AAPC Publishing
P.O. Box 23173
Shawnee Mission, Kansas 66283-0173
www.aapcpublishing.net

Publisher's Cataloging-in-Publication

Wilkins, Sheri.

   FLIPP the switch : strengthen executive function skills / Sheri Wilkins and Carol Burmeister. -- Shawnee Mission, Kansas : AAPC Publishing, [2015]

      pages ; cm.

      ISBN: 978-1-942197-01-0
      LCCN: 2014959117
      Includes bibliographical references.
      Summary: A series of practical tools for helping students strengthen their executive function skills and thereby function more successfully both personally and academically throughout life. Executive functioning involves flexibility, emotionality, impulsive control, planning and problem solving.--Publisher.

   1. Executive ability in children. 2. Executive functions (Neuropsychology) 3. Success in children. 4. Academic achievement. 5. Attention in children. 6. Problem solving in children. 7. Adaptability (Psychology) in children. 8. Impulse control disorders in children. 9. Emotional maturity. I. Burmeister, Carol Ann. II. Title.

BF723.E93 W55 2015
155.4/13--dc23   1503

Black and white art and Photographs: ©iStockphoto; www.istockphoto.com

This book is designed in Myriad Pro.

Printed in the United States of America.

Acknowledgments

Dr. Sheri Wilkins: *Deciding to write a book doesn't seem like a major decision. There's the inkling of an idea, conversations over coffee, ideas jotted down on sticky notes. At some point in time, the dream starts to take form and the real work begins.*

In 2010 my youngest son was in a car accident that resulted in a mild TBI. My friend and colleague Carol Burmeister was indefatigable in providing ideas for strategies that we could use at home to help with executive function deficits. It was this experience that led to the idea for a book that would provide parents and educators with practical strategies that could be used at home and school. I have been incredibly blessed to work with Carol, and I'm grateful for her wisdom, guidance, and patience with my idiosyncrasies.

I'd like to thank my husband, Ivan, for his unfailing support of all my wild ideas. He is my rock, and I wouldn't be who I am without him. Thank you to my children – Nathan & Brittani, Matthew & Mackenzie, Adrien & Grace, and Dominic – you four boys (and your wives) have made me the person I am today, and I'm proud to be your mom. Dominic, I'm so very proud of all the progress you have made. Thank you for letting me experiment on you with these strategies! I'd also like to thank my parents for all their love and support.

Finally, thank you to AAPC for your support of this book. Thank you to the AAPC staff members who have tirelessly answered questions and provided moral support throughout the process.

Carol Burmeister: *I am grateful to the many individuals whose support has enabled me to complete this project. I have had the opportunity to work with amazing students, their families, and educators. I am indebted to all of those who have challenged me as well as taught me.*

Dr. Sheri Wilkins is a joy to work with. She is brilliant, fun to be around, a terrific coach and mentor, and as collaborative as she is creative. During the process of writing this book, I appreciated her questions and remarks that assisted me in further developing ideas, as well as her patience with me when I lacked impulse control or flexibility of thought. Her help in enabling me to see the "big picture" as we collaborated on the manuscript was invaluable.

Dr. Sheri's son Dominic has been in my thoughts during every step of this journey. He has made tremendous progress due to his willingness to work hard and try new things.

I thank my husband, Bob, for his faith in this project and in me, and for fully supporting my passions. I am grateful to my daughter, Jennifer, as well as my sister, Janice; both of them have been great cheerleaders throughout this journey.

I appreciate Kirsten McBride's meticulous editing, and I am grateful to the AAPC staff for the care that they have invested in this book.

Foreword

Think for a minute about all of the things you need to do every morning in order to get ready for school or work. You need to wake up; get out of bed (even if you don't want to!); wash yourself; decide what to wear and dress yourself; decide what to eat and feed yourself; and finally, get out the door and to work, all in a timely fashion. Having to perform all of these tasks every morning would be overwhelming if we didn't have good executive function.

The executive functioning part of our brain works like an executive secretary, organizing our thoughts, focusing our attention on what needs to be done, helping us to avoid the many distractions in our environment. Most of us have established set routines that we carry out every morning without really thinking about it. For example, we use alarm clocks to wake up; the night before, we set out clothes to wear; and often we eat the same thing each morning. Now think for a minute how upsetting it can be if your morning routine is disrupted, like if your alarm doesn't go off at the expected time.

Now think about the distractions you might encounter during your morning routine. What if your child cries uncontrollably when it is time for you to leave? What if there is an unexpected backup in traffic on your route to work or if someone in another car cuts you off? Your executive functioning skills help you stay focused on your task without you getting hopelessly distracted or angry.

Problems in the development of cognitive skills associated with executive function are at the heart of many challenging behaviors we observe in children who struggle with organization, emotional regulation, and flexible thinking. Challenging behaviors are often symptoms of the anxiety and frustration that go hand in hand with an inability to organize and order ones own life. Dr. Ross Greene, an expert on executive function and challenging behavior, reminds us that how we think about the behavior we observe determines what we choose to do about it. When teachers and parents understand that much of the unwanted behavioral responses they observe in a child, for example, are directly tied to a lack of skills, they are more likely to choose support strategies that teach skills rather than just attempting to stop a given behavior.

This book is intended to support teachers and parents in their quest to find support strategies specifically designed to teach poor or lacking executive functioning skills. The book is beautifully simple in its design so as to offer a "crib sheet" to help teachers and parents to better understand what it means to have a problem of executive function and how to choose and carry out strategies to support the student who demonstrates such problems. The skills associated with executive function are listed along with the observable behaviors related to each particular skill. This makes it easier for educational team members to connect the specifics of behavior to the specifics of executive function. The book then takes each of the skill areas and lists five specific strategies commonly used to support that skill. Finally, each of the 25 strategies is explained using clear examples and illustrations.

Throughout much of my teaching career, I didn't have information about executive function. In retrospect, if I had access to the information presented in this book, I would have been better equipped to support my uniquely challenged students. I would have designed my classroom based on the strategies described in this book, and I am confident I would have experienced many more successes. This is one of those books you will really use; read and reread; dog-ear the pages; and fill with sticky notes and highlighted passages. This is one of those books you will really appreciate.

Kari Dunn Buron, autism education specialist/author

Table of Contents

Power Up

Do you know somebody who ...

- Is challenged with understanding the cause-and-effect relationship between his or her behavior and the reactions of others in an environment?

- Cannot successfully manage wait time, whether for an appointment at the dentist, in line for an attraction at an amusement park, to board an airplane while traveling, for a turn on the computer at home or school, for ordered food to arrive in a restaurant, for a turn to speak in a class discussion, or for a favorite television show to start?

- Exhibits excessive emotional reactions when expected to shift attention from a preferred activity to a non-preferred activity?

- Faced with a long-term school assignment or home project, has difficulty seeing the "big picture" and organizing his thinking; he may wait until the last minute to get started or attempt to complete six weeks of work in the first two days because he is not able to break the assignment or project down into manageable components and activate to work?

- Makes poor priorities when time is limited, such as watching a video game when it is time to get dressed for a family outing or talking to a classmate at the end of a class period instead of organizing materials needed for homework assignments?

- Has difficulty approaching a social setting, sizing up what is going on, and intuitively monitoring and adapting her behavior to the situation accordingly?

- Has a backpack that looks like an abandoned dumpster inside, and it is only three weeks into the school year?

- Is unable to sequence the set of behaviors necessary to complete tasks such as preparing a snack or a meal, cleaning the bathroom, completing and turning in homework, or preparing for a family or school event?

- Has difficulty regulating alertness and sustaining effort to engage in and persist with activities at home, at school, in work settings, or in the community?

How This Book Will Help

Many of the characteristics described above may be associated with deficits in executive function (EF). If any of the above challenges sound familiar to you, the information in this book can help. *FLIPP the Switch: Strengthen Executive Function Skills* is written for educators, parents and family members, and others who support students for whom executive function is a challenge. It will provide assistance in understanding the challenges of EF deficits and, most important, present strategies that can be used immediately to address some of the most common EF challenges. All of the strategies are designed to be easily replicated by educational professionals as well as parents of children who have EF deficits.

When it comes to selecting strategies to support students with EF deficits, it is important to consider practices whose effectiveness is backed by research. Evidence of efficacy in practice include those that generate specific behavioral and developmental outcomes for students, have been established in the applied research literature, and can be effectively implemented in school, home, vocational and community environments (Odom, Boyd, Hall, & Hume, 2010). All of the strategies in this book have a strong research base, and citations to that effect are included throughout the book.

Organization of the Book

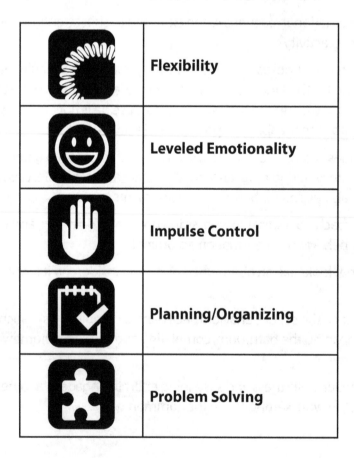

	Flexibility
	Leveled Emotionality
	Impulse Control
	Planning/Organizing
	Problem Solving

FLIPP the Switch: Strengthen Executive Function Skills consists of two main sections. The first outlines the FLIPP model, what EF challenges look like and how they are manifested, how EF deficits impact learning and behavior, and disorders that commonly manifest EF deficits. The remainder of the book is organized around the FLIPP model, with chapters about each of the following FLIPP components: flexibility, leveled emotionality, impulse control, planning, and problem solving.

Each chapter details strategies that can be used by both educators and parents. The treatment of each strategy consists of a description of the function of the strategy or tool, detailed directions for when and how to use the strategy, instructions on how to make the tool, and a template (if appropriate) to help educators and parents make their own.

The tools that are described in the book are as follows:

- Flexibility
    - Visual Scales
    - Wait Card
    - Countdown Timer
    - Power Card
    - SOARR (Specify, Observe, Analyze, Respond, Reflect)

- Leveled Emotionality
    - Choice Cards
    - Calming Routines
    - Help and Break Cue Cards
    - Chunking
    - Social Narratives: Story Format

- Impulse Control
    - Positive Behavior Interventions and Supports (PBIS)
    - Reminder Cards
    - Reinforcement Systems
    - Social Autopsies
    - Cognitive Scripts

- Planning/Organizing
    - First-Then Boards
    - Video Modeling
    - Organizing: Master Binder System
    - Contingency Mapping
    - Project Mapping

- Problem Solving
    - Work Systems
    - Checklists
    - Task Analysis
    - Priming
    - Metacognitive Problem Solving

FLIPP the Switch: Strengthen Executive Function Skills is intended to help educational professionals as well as parents gain insight into the social, academic, and behavioral challenges of students with EF deficits and to provide them with practical tools to empower their students or children to develop the strong EF skills necessary for success in all environments.

Note. The term "student" as used in the following refers to individuals of all ages, and is used for the sake of clarity and simplification. The pronouns "he" and "she" are alternated for the same reason.

Part 1

Introduction
to
Executive Function

What Is Executive Function (EF)?

Think about the CEO of a large Fortune 500 company. He (or she) has numerous things going on at any given time. There are meetings to attend, projects to plan, and details to attend to and remember. How does one person stay organized enough to get it all done efficiently? The reality is that most CEOs have an executive or administrative assistant who takes care of the details, ensuring that the CEO is at the right place at the right time, with the right materials at hand. The administrative assistant is the one who pays attention to the details and plans, organizes, and manages time and space.

Executive function is similar to the "administrative assistant" in the previous paragraph. EF refers to a collection of mental processes that assist a person in organizing, planning, problem solving, and paying attention to and remembering details. In addition, strong EF skills help us to remain calm under pressure and to be flexible when things do not work out right the first time. Figure 1 lists the major components of EF.

	Flexibility	The ability to change your mind and make changes to your plans as needed
	Leveled Emotionality	The ability to emotionally self-regulate and avoid extensive mood swings
	Impulse Control	The ability to control your impulses, such as waiting to speak until called upon
	Planning/Organizing	The ability to make plans and keep track of time and materials so that work is finished on time
	Problem Solving	The ability to know when there is a problem that needs to be solved, generate solutions, select one, and evaluate the outcome

Figure 1. Executive function components.

What Do EF Challenges Look Like?

Common challenges for a student with EF deficits include planning and prioritizing, completing tasks, sustaining effort, storing information in working memory and then recalling that information, seeking more information if needed, regulating alertness, and adapting to changes. The manifestation of EF challenges is unique to each student. Whether mild, moderate, or severe, EF challenges significantly affect everyday functioning at school, work, community, and home (Coyne & Rood, 2011), even when motivation and intellectual abilities are high.

Completing most tasks requires the successful orchestration of several types of EF skills. In most real-life situations, these functions are not entirely distinct. They work together to produce competent executive functioning (Center on the Developing Child at Harvard University, 2011).

Figure 2 lists common challenges seen in individuals with EF deficits. Students with EF deficits may experience difficulties with working memory (WM), which is the ability to hold information and use information over brief time periods without using memory aids or cues (Best & Miller, 2010). Difficulties with WM can interact with, and influence, the other challenges, as an inability to remember and activate information may exacerbate other deficits. For example, a student who encounters difficulty with a challenging math problem . . .

1. Needs to seek the initiative to ask for help.

2. In doing so, he needs to inhibit his impulse to call out to the teacher for help, remembering to raise his hand and wait for the teacher to come to him.

3. Once the teacher is available and approaches the student to offer support, he needs to remember his specific question and focus on asking the question articulately.

4. Once he has received an answer, he needs to utilize his working memory and access recall in order to complete the question.

Any breakdown in these processes may lead to a feeling of frustration, which could result in an angry response.

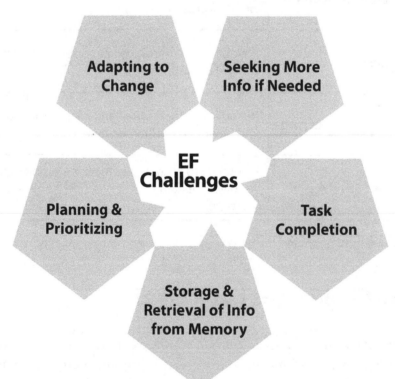

Figure 2. Common EF challenges.

Not all students who have difficulty with EF experience all of the challenges listed above. Each person has relative strengths as well as relative weaknesses. It is important to concentrate on a student's strengths, as well as implement specific strategies to support the EF challenges she is exhibiting.

How Are EF Challenges Manifested?

. . .

Ahmed's mother is at the end of her rope. She received another phone call from her son's teacher today, informing her that he failed to turn in his homework (again) and that he had told the teacher that he didn't know where his "stupid homework" was. Ahmed's teacher thinks that he might need to be retained in the second grade if he cannot change his negative attitude and become more responsible and respectful. It's apparent that Ahmed is a smart boy; after all, he learned to read when he was 4 and he is a whiz with numbers. If he would just learn how to organize himself and get things done, on time, and turned in, he could really succeed in school. It also wouldn't hurt if he would learn to mind his manners and not say every rude thing that pops into his head. Maybe his teacher is right; if he is retained, he'll learn to behave himself and he'll want to improve.

. . .

Executive function challenges can affect a student in many areas, both at home and in school. As Figure 3 illustrates, a student with EF difficulties may find it tough to achieve in school, not because of a lack of effort or desire to do well but due to a lack of the necessary skills. Often these students are seen as unmotivated or behaviorally challenged. However, it is important to differentiate between "won't" and "can't." Although it may seem as though a student could meet expectations if she wanted to, but doesn't do so because she simply won't, perhaps the reality is that she lacks the skills to do what is expected and, therefore, cannot meet the expectations without support.

Additionally, many students with EF deficits exhibit slow processing speeds, which may look like resistance or stubbornness, when the student may simply be working through what behaviors are required in the situation.

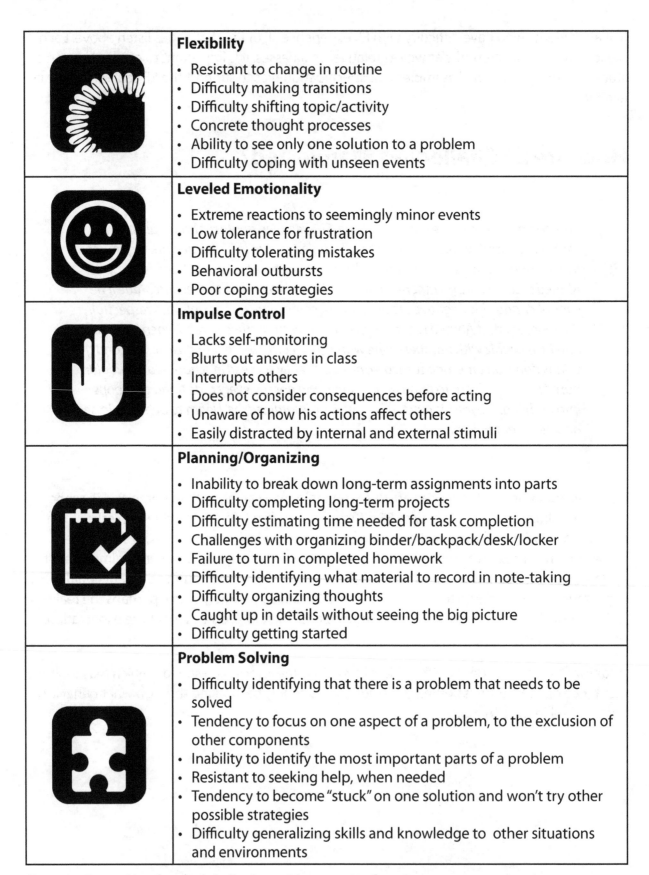

	Flexibility
	• Resistant to change in routine • Difficulty making transitions • Difficulty shifting topic/activity • Concrete thought processes • Ability to see only one solution to a problem • Difficulty coping with unseen events
	Leveled Emotionality
	• Extreme reactions to seemingly minor events • Low tolerance for frustration • Difficulty tolerating mistakes • Behavioral outbursts • Poor coping strategies
	Impulse Control
	• Lacks self-monitoring • Blurts out answers in class • Interrupts others • Does not consider consequences before acting • Unaware of how his actions affect others • Easily distracted by internal and external stimuli
	Planning/Organizing
	• Inability to break down long-term assignments into parts • Difficulty completing long-term projects • Difficulty estimating time needed for task completion • Challenges with organizing binder/backpack/desk/locker • Failure to turn in completed homework • Difficulty identifying what material to record in note-taking • Difficulty organizing thoughts • Caught up in details without seeing the big picture • Difficulty getting started
	Problem Solving
	• Difficulty identifying that there is a problem that needs to be solved • Tendency to focus on one aspect of a problem, to the exclusion of other components • Inability to identify the most important parts of a problem • Resistant to seeking help, when needed • Tendency to become "stuck" on one solution and won't try other possible strategies • Difficulty generalizing skills and knowledge to other situations and environments

Figure 3. Examples of typical challenges with executive functions.

The Phone Call That Every Parent of a Teenager Dreads Receiving

My phone rang as I was making a presentation to a group of parents and teachers of students with disabilities. I considered not answering it, but decided I could take a moment for a quick call. "Mom, I've been in a car accident, but I think I'm okay." Hearing these words, my heart dropped and I had a moment of panic as I tried to decide what to do with the group of people waiting for me to start the presentation. One of my colleagues stepped in and took over, and I headed home to evaluate the situation with my 17-year-old son.

After a long night that included a trip to Urgent Care and frequent awakenings throughout the night to check for concussion effects, we felt we had very fortunately avoided a serious problem. However, within a few weeks we began to notice behavioral changes in our son. For several months, we thought that he was simply going through a rough time and that he was choosing to be difficult. He slept a great deal of the time, argued constantly, made outrageous (and often extremely embarrassing and graphic) statements out loud, struggled with initiating and sustaining activity, and engaged in dangerous and unsafe activities.

It took some time before we finally saw a pediatric neuro-psychologist, who assessed our son and informed us that he was exhibiting the effects of a mild traumatic brain injury (TBI). She explained that his memory (particularly working and short-term memory) and EF skills had been greatly affected, along with his overall cognitive abilities.

Needless to say, we were devastated. We envisioned a future in which our son would not be able to live independently due to his inability to plan and problem solve, along with his impulsive behavior and angry outbursts. We watched as his friends from high school stopped coming around and he dealt with the loneliness that ensued as others responded to him with shock and negativity. We realized we needed help to support him in functioning in an age-appropriate and societally acceptable manner.

It was largely that search for strategies that would help him to navigate the expectations of a young adult in modern society that resulted in the writing of this book. As a parent and an educator, I hoped to help not only our family but other families as well.

– Sheri Wilkins

How Do EF Deficits Impact Learning and Behavior?

Executive function deficits impact almost every aspect of learning and behavior. **Every day, all day, in every situation, we are called on to self-regulate behavior.**

Take a typical day for a middle school student. She needs to:

1. Wake up on time

2. Plan grooming activities that don't take too long but still get the job done

3. Choose clothing that is appropriate for the temperature outside and the school setting

4. Leave the house early enough to make it to school on time

5. Walk/ride/bicycle to school, arriving with enough time to get to the first class before the tardy bell rings

During the school day, she must:

1. Listen to the teacher

2. Keep track of time and finish her work on time

3. Ask for help when needed

4. Meaningfully include her prior knowledge in discussions

5. Engage appropriately in groups, and wait to speak until she is called upon

6. Be flexible enough to go with the new plan when something changes in the schedule

7. Control her emotions and use strategies to avoid an emotional outburst if the new plan is frustrating, or something doesn't go her way during the day

When she returns home, she must:

1. Use all these skills as she (a) does her chores, (b) finishes her homework, and (c) interacts with her family and/or friends

As illustrated, EF is an extremely important part of being successful in life. If someone is inflexible, any kind of change in the plan or routine can cause insurmountable problems. This can lead to emotional outbursts, or *lability*, which is a condition of excessive emotional reactions and frequent mood changes. People around an emotionally labile person may feel as though they are "walking on egg shells." When someone is impulsive, she may act without thinking or planning, sometimes leading to dangerous or unpredictable situations. Likewise, a lack of planning may lead to poor results or an inability to finish a task on time. Finally, difficulty with problem solving can result in difficulty looking at a task from several angles and choosing a solution to a problem that makes sense and leads to a positive outcome. When things don't work out as expected, an inability to problem-solve can lead to frustration and giving up. In addition, people with EF challenges often struggle with working memory, the ability to temporarily retain information in order to solve a problem or complete a task. Working memory deficits can exacerbate and contribute to the challenges presented by other EF problems.

Which Disorders Commonly Manifest Executive Function Deficits?

The *Diagnostic and Statistical Manual of Mental Disorders* (DSM) provides a common language and standard criteria for the classification of mental disorders. Several of the clinical conditions described in the DSM-5 (American Psychiatric Association, 2013) – the fifth edition – reflect some form of executive dysfunction. For example, disorders such as attention deficit disorders, autism, fetal alcohol syndrome disorder, intellectual disability, obsessive compulsive disorders, social communication disorder, specific learning disability, Tourette's Syndrome, and traumatic brain injury are often understood to have a component of EF deficits (Attwood, 2014; Barkley, 1997; Benton, 2001; Channon, Pratt, & Robertson, 2003; Danielsson, Henry, Rönnberg, & Nilsson 2010; Green et al., 2009; McDonald et al., 2014; Watkins et al., 2005). In addition, individuals with diagnoses such as anxiety, depression, and schizophrenia may exhibit deficits in the area of executive function (Channon & Green, 1999; Eysenck, Derakshan, Santos, & Calvo, 2007; Hoff & Kremen, 2003).

Figure 4 shows some common conditions that are typified by challenges with executive function skills (sometimes referred to as executive dysfunction).

Executive function deficits are strongly associated with components of:		
Attention Deficit Disorders	Anxiety	Autism
Depression	Fetal Alcohol Syndrome Disorder	Intellectual Disability
Obsessive Compulsive Disorders	Schizophrenia	Social Communication Disorder
Specific Learning Disability	Tourette's Syndrome	Traumatic Brain Injury

Figure 4. Medical and neurological conditions that may evidence challenges with executive function.

A student does not have to have a disability to have challenges with executive functions. He can be bright, creative, capable, and talented, yet significantly impaired in his ability to set realistic goals, adapt to changing circumstances, persist at solving problems, hold onto and work with information, and recognize his emotions as well as those of others.

Part 2

Strategies to Strengthen Executive Function Skills

Flexibility

**The ability to change your mind and
make changes to your plans as needed**

Visual Scales

. . .

Dieter had a hard time monitoring his vocal volume to match a specific situation. When his teachers reminded him to use his "inside" or his "outside" voice, he didn't seem to understand that there was a difference. Whether he wanted to speak to a peer buddy who sat directly next to him, to the cafeteria proctor who monitored his table at lunch, or to the principal as she made a daily visit to Dieter's classroom, he usually shouted his words. Dieter's parents shared that the same thing occurred in other settings. For example, Dieter shouted his food order in a restaurant, in church services he shouted hymns instead of singing them, and even at home, he often spoke in an inappropriately loud voice to family members who were close-by.

Adults who support Dieter verbally prompted him to use vocal volume that was appropriate for the situation but with little success. To make the idea of vocal volume concrete for Dieter, and to help him understand that there was more than one level of vocal volume and that he needed to be flexible in using appropriate vocal volume, a visual scale was created (see Figure 5). The words "too loud," "just right," and "too soft" were used as comparisons for vocal volume. A bead was attached to the scale that could be moved up and down to indicate vocal volume that was appropriate for the situation. When Dieter's vocal volume was inappropriate, the adults who supported Dieter used the scale, moving the bead to indicate the level of volume that was appropriate for the situation. Dieter soon learned how to monitor his voice level according to the situation.

. . .

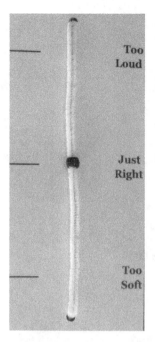

Figure 5. Example of a visual scale used to teach vocal volume.

Students who have difficulty being flexible often have very concrete thought processes. Visual scales are illustrations of social behaviors, emotions, and abstract ideas (Coffin & Smith, 2009), and can be used to address concrete thought processes by visually representing concepts that may be challenging for a student. Used successfully with students from kindergarten through high school, visual scales can help examine and explain many social concepts and social behaviors (Buron & Curtis, 2012). For example, a child can modulate his emotions by communicating to a parent that she is anxious by indicating a high level of stress on a scale that rates levels of anxiety; similarly, an educator might use a rating scale to signify to a student that his talking exceeds the maximum loudness level that is allowed in the classroom (Jaime & Knowlton, 2007).

• • •

Jeremiah showed no hesitation when approaching another student and beginning to talk about his latest subject of interest. He did not understand that not everyone he approached was interested in hearing every single fact there was to know about snakes – his current special interest. He would approach someone, stand face to face just a few inches away from him, and then begin talking. If the other student backed away, Jeremiah simply moved forward to fill in the space. Jeremiah's parents, teachers, and even some of his peers, attempted to te John-Paul *appropriate physical proximity to another pers gestures and verbally prompting him, but these strategies did not work.*

A visual scale was created as a visual continuum to teach Jeremiah how to use appropriate physical proximity during social exchanges, not just when talking with somebody about his subject of interest (see Figure 6) but also for other situations that involved conversing with others, such as trying to gain the teacher's attention to ask a question in class, having a conversation with another student about the school assembly, approaching a visitor who has entered the school office, etc.

• • •

The scale was designed using the words "close" and "far apart" as comparisons for physical proximity. A list of concrete behaviors representing each number on the scale was developed to help Jeremiah understand how to rate his physical proximity and when and where to use each physical proximity level.

5 = Being far apart from someone (e.g., playing a game on the playground with someone that requires us to be at opposite ends of the playground; being at the front of a line of 100 spectators waiting to get into a sporting event would be far away from the person at the end of the line)

4 = Being far enough away that I need to get a person's attention before attempting to talk to him (e.g., sitting at my desk in a classroom, my teacher may be at the back of the room, so rather than shouting, I raise my hand to ask the teacher a question)

3 = About one arm's length apart from the person I am talking to (e.g., discussing what we did over the weekend with a friend; approaching someone I don't know to introduce myself; when approaching someone to ask for help in the grocery store)

2 = Close enough to easily touch someone and talk quietly (e.g., standing in line in the cafeteria; asking the student with the locker next to mine if I can borrow a textbook)

1 = Very close (e.g., whispering to someone or having a very private conversation)

A copy of the scale, with the behaviors corresponding to the numbers listed on the back, was given to the educators who support Jeremiah, his two assigned peer buddies, and his parents. When Jeremiah got too close to someone during a conversation, those supporting him pointed to the number that represented the appropriate physical proximity the situation called for. Jeremiah soon learned that a "3" was appropriate for most conversational exchanges.

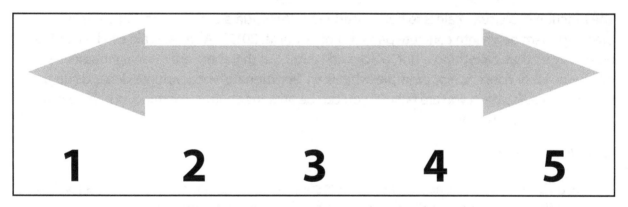

Figure 6. Visual scale used to provide a visual breakdown of behaviors or concepts.

• • •

Shaniqua had difficulty coping with unforeseen events. Though the educators who support her did their best to forewarn her when there was a change in plans at school, she was not always prepared ahead of time for modifications or adjustments, such as the appearance of a substitute teacher, a change in the assembly schedule, or a change in menu items in the cafeteria from what was posted on the lunch menu calendar.

A visual scale was created with the numbers from 1 to 5, each number representing the behaviors described below. Shaniqua was taught how to use the scale in school environments to express her anxiety level and monitor her behavior. Data indicate that Shaniqua has become much more flexible when there is a change in routine or when other unforeseen events occur.

5 = I am totally stressed and feel a meltdown coming on – I need a break to calm down.

4 = I am mad and angry. This is really hard for me. I will need lots of help to handle it.

3 = I am getting frustrated, and I might put my head down for a minute.

2 = I am a little anxious about the change of plans, but I can put it on my schedule and I think I will be okay.

1 = I am feeling calm. I know I can handle this on my own.

• • •

Make a Visual Scale

Function:

The function of a visual scale is to help a student better understand abstract concepts by breaking them down into concrete parts (Buron & Curtis, 2012). A visual scale can be used to demonstrate that everything is not "black and white," but that there are often various levels of a behavior or concept. For example, what is an "appropriate" vocal volume depends on the circumstances in which you are talking; you can be anxious about something, but there can be different levels of anxiety.

When/How to Use:

- Use a visual scale any time a student needs support in understanding the various levels of a behavior. It can be used in the home, at school, in community settings.

- Use it to communicate a desired change of behavior. Noise level can be a very difficult concept to communicate because it is often relative. For instance, the noise level that is acceptable on a walk outdoors is usually different from the acceptable noise level walking through a museum. With a visual scale, the current behavior can be given a number ("Your noise level is at a 4 right now") and the desired level can be identified ("You need to be at a level 2").

- Use a card with either words or numbers; the important thing is to have some way of indicating a high level versus a low level. The adult supporting the student reflects the current level of the behavior by sliding the bead to the appropriate level ("Your voice is too loud right now") and indicates the desired level by pointing ("Your voice needs to be here – where it says 'Just Right'").

- As the behavior changes, move the bead (if appropriate) accordingly to reflect the new level.

- Use the visual scale to promote self-monitoring. Students can use the visual scale to check in on their own behavior, emotions, and effects on their immediate environment (Jaime & Knowlton, 2007).

- Collect data to measure the effectiveness of the visual scale strategy. Depending on the behavior that is being targeted, use the data to determine whether the strategy is effectively increasing desired behavior or decreasing interfering behavior.

How to Make:

- Print out the desired visual scale (see Figures 7 and 8) on cardstock.

- Cut out the visual scale from the template.

- Laminate all pieces.

- Use a hole punch to make a hole at the top dot and a hole at the bottom dot.

- String a bead on a pipe cleaner and thread one end through the top hole and the other end through the bottom hole. Bend the ends and add tape to hold the pipe cleaner in place.

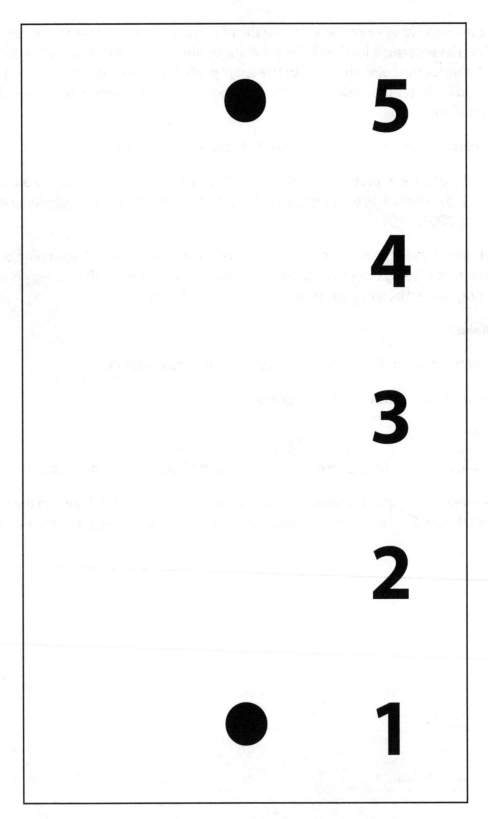

Figure 7. Visual scale template.

Figure 8. Visual scale template for vocal volume.

Wait Card

. . .

Jackson and Jillian were excited about their upcoming trip to the museum, which was featuring a special exhibit on robotic technology, a subject that interests both of them. Their dad had planned to take them to the exhibit on a school vacation day. Getting up early that morning, Jackson and Jillian were ready to go when Dad got a phone call from his supervisor at work. Something had come up that would need a few minutes of Dad's attention as he took care of some business through email correspondence.

Dad told his children that they had to wait for 10 minutes. Knowing from past experience that he might be barraged with questions from his children, such as "How long do we have to wait?" "Has it been 10 minutes yet?" "How much longer?," that would distract him from what he needed to do, he used visual strategies to help them manage their wait time behavior.

He set out a wait card and told them that they had a choice of writing in their journal about what they expected to see at the museum or playing a card game of "Go Fish." He then set their Time Timer®, a visual tool that is useful in all environments to help children understand the concept of elapsed time, for 10 minutes. Jackson and Jillian used the wait time appropriately. Dad finished his correspondence, they had a successful visit to the museum, and Dad reinforced their appropriate wait time behavior by treating them to ice cream on the way home.

. . .

Waiting is an inevitable part of life, and learning to wait is an essential skill for both academic and social success. For a student who has difficulty shifting focus or activities, making transitions, coping with unforeseen events, and other behaviors requiring flexibility, having to wait can be especially challenging and may result in inappropriate behaviors.

Waiting has to do with time, and concepts related to time are abstract and can be difficult for many students. For example, if the student has not mastered the skill of telling time, saying, "You have a few minutes," "Hang on a second," or "I'll be ready to leave in a minute" may be confusing (Myles & Kolar, 2013; Myles, Trautman, & Schelvan, 2013). On the other hand, a student who does have time telling skills may take "Just a minute" literally and be equally confused, although for a different reason.

In teaching students what to do while waiting, one of the most important strategies adults can use is to **model appropriate wait time behavior.** Shouting at an automated system when put on hold while trying to get through to a live person in customer service when making a phone call, honking the car horn repeatedly when stuck in traffic, continually frowning at and asking the receptionist when the doctor will see you, expressing frustration when the web access on your "high-speed" Internet connection takes more than a few seconds are not examples of how to wait that we want our children or students to emulate.

Another strategy that is essential to teaching expected wait time behavior is to **acknowledge and reinforce appropriate waiting behavior** that we observe in our children or students. In addition, we can support students who struggle with waiting by providing answers to three questions:

1. "What does it mean to wait?"
2. "How long should I wait?"
3. "What should I do?"

[handwritten note: what does it mean to wait?: first, then long.]

"What Does It Mean to Wait?"

The first question we need to answer when teaching students how to wait is "What does it mean to wait?" We can do this by defining wait time and helping the student recognize times when she might be expected to wait. Minahan (2013) suggests giving a "cheat sheet" with clues to help students recognize what's going on around them and providing a list of common phrases that denote waiting. For example, "When you hear someone say 'hang on,' 'wait,' 'hold on a moment,' or 'just a second,' this means you are expected to wait." Teach about sequences in a variety of situations or routines where waiting may be required; for example, at a red-light traffic signal, *first* we wait, and *then* we go when the light turns green; at the dentist's office, *first* we wait, and *then* we see the dentist; during P.E. at school, *first* we wait until the teacher finishes roll call, and *then* we start our warm-up exercises; during conversations with somebody, *first* we wait for the other person to finish speaking, and *then* we speak.

[handwritten note: ex.]

"How Long Should I Wait?"

[handwritten note: be specific when responding to time related questions]

The second question that is important to answer is "How long should I wait?" Be specific when responding to time-related questions. "Until the bell rings, the time on the clock indicates time is up, or the timer signals the end"; "until I finish putting away the dishes"; "until the end of the song or video"; "until the nurse calls us from the waiting area"; "until your number is called"; "until the server brings our food," etc., are ways to let somebody know that wait time has an end. Timers, such as sand timers, kitchen timers, and the Time Timer® (a tool that can be used as a quiet visual countdown as well as for helping students gain an understanding of the concept of elapsed time) can be used in the home, school, and community environments to give meaning to the concept of wait time and help students comprehend how long they might wait. Visual timers can be especially helpful as concrete reminders of a set amount of time and to establish duration.

"What Should I Do?"

The final question to answer specifically is "What should I do?" A list of activities for students to do while they wait can help them manage wait time. Consider the age of the student, the environment in which he is expected to wait, and his interests. Examples of activities and strategies to support students while they wait include the following:

- For a preschooler who is waiting at a doctor's office for an appointment, look at photos on a parent's iPhone, engage in quiet phonemic awareness activities with parent ("What words rhyme with 'bear'? 'dog'? 'cat'?"), read a picture book.

- For a child who is waiting for a special occasion to arrive that is weeks away, provide a calendar that displays the occasion and mark off each day leading up to it.

- For a child who is waiting for a food order to arrive in a busy restaurant, play tic-tac-toe, estimate how much the bill will be for the meal, listen to music on digital device using headphones.

- For an elementary school student who is waiting for a turn on the playground swings, count to 100, play a hand game such as rock-paper-scissors with the person next to him in line.

- For a middle school student who is waiting in a long line to purchase lunch in the cafeteria, silently name a proper noun for each letter of the alphabet, read the nutritional posters on the wall.

- For a high school student who has finished his assignments prior to the transition time to the next activity, read a library book, draw on a notepad, review homework assignments in binder.

- For a teenager who is waiting for a friend to arrive for a scheduled visit, use the wait time to practice a musical instrument, tidy up her bedroom, read a library book, make sketches on a drawing pad, review long-term homework assignments in school binder.

Wait time activities can be paired with a visual support in the form of a visual cue card to assist students in understanding what to do while waiting. For example, a high school student struggled with waiting at the orthodontist's office. His parents gave him a list of activities to engage in while he waited, as well as a cue card (in the form of a small card he kept in his wallet and took out as needed) as a visual support (see Figure 9).

While waiting for my appointment at the orthodontist, I can:

1. Complete a crossword puzzle in one of Dr. Lowenstein's magazines.

2. Check out the aquarium in the waiting room to see if there are any new fish.

3. Read my *Car and Driver* magazine.

Figure 9. Visual support for expected behaviors while waiting at the orthodontist's office.

In another example, a student walked around the classroom and bothered other students when she needed help in her math class. Her instructional assistant developed a visual support to cue the student as to which activities she could engage in while waiting for help (see Figure 10).

While waiting for assistance in math class, I can:

1. Do the problems I am able to do on my own.

2. Start tonight's homework.

3. Review lessons from last week.

Figure 10. Visual support illustrating expected behaviors while waiting for help in the classroom.

A **wait card** is another effective visual support strategy (Wong et al., 2013) that provides a concrete cue to help support demonstration of appropriate wait time behaviors (see Figure 11). Using a wait card gives a *beginning* (e.g., the card is handed to the student or set within view; the student can also be prompted to access wait card from her desk or backpack) and an *end* (the card is picked up or put away) to wait time. Adults can also use the wait card to cue an entire group (e.g., in a classroom or school cafeteria, at Scout meetings, or in the home to cue siblings) while responding to a student's urgent need for attention.

Figure 11. Wait card. The Picture Communication Symbols ©1981-2005 by Mayer-Johnson LLC. All Rights Reserved Worldwide. Used with permission.

We can support a student in learning and using behaviors that he is expected to use while waiting by proactively teaching wait time behavior. Find opportunities to ask the student to wait, let him know what the expected behaviors are, and pair the verbal instruction with a wait card as well as another visual card to illustrate wait time behavior if necessary. When a student has demonstrated appropriate wait time behaviors for a short time, gradually increase the wait time, using a system to reinforce expected behaviors.

Some students have a desire to "complete" anything they start before going on to the next scheduled task or activity. We can also use the wait card strategy to teach them that it is okay to wait and come back to the task or activity later.

How to Teach:

Show the student the wait card and teach the wait card strategy in a 1:1 instructional setting prior to actually using it.

1. Have the student begin the task/activity, ensuring he is calm.

2. Tell the student she needs to complete the task/activity at a later time.

3. Place a visible support indicating "Wait" on the work in progress.

4. Reinforce the student for using appropriate wait time behavior.

5. Gradually increase the "wait" time to the next day or task/activity time.

For students for whom waiting is a challenge, teaching wait skills can be a proactive approach to reducing or preventing interfering behaviors such as disturbing others, getting up and wandering around, or making inappropriate noises that may occur as a result of having to wait while increasing social competence, flexibility, impulse control, and engagement in other on-task behaviors.

The strategies described in this section for teaching wait skills are effective across age ranges and environments. Support the teaching of successful use of wait time by incorporating these strategies with other strategies outlined in this book such as reinforcement, video modeling, social narratives, choice cards, and first-then (a useful tool to help prepare students that they might not get what they desire immediately).

Make a Wait Card

Function:

The function of the wait card is to support the student in demonstrating appropriate wait time behavior.

When/How to Use:

- At home, provide as a visual cue to help manage wait time. For example, a child has asked to use the home computer while his sibling is using it. Use the wait card and a timer to let him know when his turn will come.

- In school environments, provide as a visual cue to help manage wait time. For example, when a student is asked to wait her turn, wait for an activity, wait in line, etc., she may be given a wait card. Let the student know the expected behaviors associated with the use of the wait card. A student may have a list of wait time activities, such as those described following the title "What Should I Do?" on pages 25-26. The wait card can also be used to let a student know that it is okay to leave a non-completed task or activity and come back to finish it later. For example, place a wait card on top of work in progress to let a student know that she will need to complete the task at a later time.

- In the community, provide as a visual cue to manage wait time while waiting for appointments, to be served at the DMV office, to board an airplane, etc. Cards may be carried by the students for whom they are created or by adults who support them and presented as needed.

- Collect data to measure the effectiveness of the wait card strategy. Use the data to determine whether the strategy is effective in helping the student demonstrate appropriate wait time behaviors.

How to Make:

- Using a piece of cardstock, reproduce the "wait" template (Figure 12). Other ideas for a wait card include having a photo of the word "wait" on the parent's or student's tablet, smartphone, or attached to a keychain. The word "wait" can also be written or reproduced on a small card such as a business card.

- Laminate the template, if possible, fold in the middle to create a sign, and place where waiting is required and/or where a student and/or those who support her will have access to it (e.g., inside a homework view binder, student desk, backpack, purse; on a classroom whiteboard rail or counter at home).

Template:

Figure 12. Wait card template. The Picture Communication Symbols ©1981-2005 by Mayer-Johnson LLC. All Rights Reserved Worldwide. Used with permission.

Countdown Timer

· · ·

Lydia thrived in her school program, well accustomed to the routine and structure. When a change in schedule occurred, she was usually able to demonstrate flexibility, as long as her teachers could indicate the time duration for the activities that were the cause of each schedule change. Fire drills, however, were a challenge, because no absolute time was allotted for that activity. Lydia had no idea how long she would need to remain outside with her classmates, and she couldn't understand why her teacher couldn't tell exactly what time they could re-enter their classroom.

Using a countdown timer, Lydia's teachers were able to count down, pulling off numbers 5 through 1, indicating that time was passing and that eventually the fire drill would end and they could return to the classroom. Having a visual support helped structure that undefined period of time for Lydia and enabled her to be more flexible while she waited for the fire drill to end.

· · ·

"When will I be finished?""How much do I have to do?""When do I make the next transition?""How long do we have to stay out here before the fire drill is over?""How long do I have to wait in the dentist's office?"Visual countdown timers help place boundaries on open-ended activities such as these, and are especially useful for those situations when adults can't control specifically "how long." When using a visual countdown timer, no specific time increment is used, which makes this a helpful tool if the timing of an activity or transition needs to be flexible (Hume, 2008).

You can create your own visual timer using free downloadable materials (http://www.icontalk.com/downloads.html) that Barbara Bloomfield, speech-language pathologist, consultant for autism spectrum disorder, and director of Icon Talk, a firm dedicated to the development and distribution of communication-based visual teaching materials, shares on her website, or you can use the template provided in Figure 17.

To use the timer, take the numbers off at intervals and place them in the "all done" pocket (see pages 33-34). State, "Now you have four,""Now you have three," etc., continuing to use the number cards until All Done. The beauty of this timer is that we as adults can control the length of time between moving the number cards. Though we may not know how long we have to wait outside until the fire drill is over, the assembly will end, the photographer will take the class picture, the late bus will arrive, etc., we have a way to let the student understand that time is passing and that there will be an end to the situation.

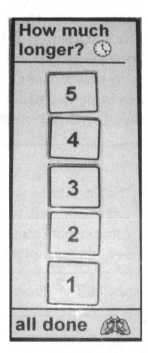

Figure 13. Example of a countdown timer. The Picture Communication Symbols ©1981-2005 by Mayer-Johnson LLC. All Rights Reserved Worldwide. Used with permission.

. . .

Teresa has been attending the choir class at her middle school as one of her electives and for the opportunity for mainstreaming that it provides. As the holiday season approaches, plans are made for a special holiday performance. Teresa's teachers know that Teresa is very concrete and has a need to know when a situation will end. Teresa's choir teacher constructs a countdown timer and positions herself where Teresa can see her during the performance. The teacher knows how many musical numbers will be performed. She uses the timer (see Figure 13) to represent the passage of time so that Teresa can see that there is an end in sight.

. . .

The authors have used this tool with students of all ages, from preschool through high school. Parents report success with this strategy also. Barbara Bloomfield (2009) shares a hospital emergency room story during which this strategy was used, where a child had what seemed to be an endless wait to have his knee stitched up. Though the child was distressed to be in what to him was an unpleasant environment, he was aware that the time would come when he could leave that environment; Mom's use of the timer also let him know that she was aware of his distress, helping to reduce his anxiety.

Effective visual supports include objects within a student's environment that support engagement in a desired behavior or skill, independent of prompts (Wong et al., 2013). As a visual support, visual timers can be useful for students who have difficulty staying on task or transitioning (Aspy & Grossman, 2012). In addition to the countdown timer, other visual timers can be used in many environments to provide cues or reminders related to the concept of time. Physical timers may be purchased in a variety of sizes. Apps are available for the iPhone/iPad and for Android devices. A couple of options are listed below (see Figures 14, 15, and 16).

Time Timer®

The Time Timer® is one of the most popular visual timers available. The interface is simple and uncluttered, and it offers silent operation with an optional audible alert. Time Timers® come in three sizes (3," 8," and 12") and as an app for the iPhone or iPad or Android devices. See http://www.timetimer.com

---

Figure 14. Time Timer®.

Kiddie Countdown Timer

The Kiddie Countdown Timer is an iPhone or iPad app that may be downloaded free of charge from the Apple AppStore. It features simple and clear graphics in green, yellow, and red to visually display how much time is left. For Android users, try Kids Timer, which can be downloaded free of charge from Google Play.

Figure 15. Kiddie Countdown Timer.

Touch and Go Visual Countdown Timer

This countdown timer may be set for various times (in seconds), and the image to be displayed during the countdown and sound to play when time is up may be personalized. See http://www.touch-and-go.org

---

Figure16. Touch and Go Visual Countdown Timer.

Make a Countdown Timer

Function:

The function of the countdown timer is to help structure undefined periods of time.

When/How to Use:

- Use the timer any time the question of "How much longer?" or "When will I be finished?" arises in home, school, or community settings.

- Use it to place boundaries on open-ended activities. For example: when waiting for a medical appointment, when waiting for ordered food to arrive in a restaurant, to show how much longer a student needs to work or play, to show how much longer the class will have to stay outside until returning to class after the fire drill, etc.

- Place the numbers on the card in descending order. The adult supporting the student reflects the passage of time, arbitrarily assigning time increments to each of the five numbers. Each number might represent 5 minutes or 1 minute, etc. Take the numbers off at intervals, keeping the increments constant if possible. Say, "Now you have four"; then "Now you have three," etc., until the final number is removed and the activity is over.

- Collect data to record how the student uses the countdown timer strategy.

How to Make:

- Print the countdown strip and one set of numbers on cardstock (see Figure 17).

- Cut out all pieces.

- Laminate all pieces.

- Using the "hard" side, place Velcro® pieces on the back of each number.

- Using the "soft" side, place 5 Velcro® pieces on the countdown strip to hold the numbers.

- Tape an envelope to the back of the card to hold the numbers when using the timer.

Template:

Figure 17. Countdown timer. LessonPix; www.lessonpix.com ©2014-2015 by LessonPix. All Rights Reserved. Used with permission.

Power Card

• • •

Caroline, a middle school student, had difficulty participating successfully during group activities at school, especially in classroom settings. In her Spanish class, learner expectations for participating successfully as part of a group included transitioning from lecture to group activities, being prepared by having the appropriate materials ready, taking turns in discussions, staying on topic during discussions, and considering the points of view of other group members. Once the students were excused to work in their groups, Caroline often exhibited undesirable behaviors, including wandering around the room instead of joining her group when the teacher signaled the transition, as well as interrupting others during group discussion.

Knowing that Caroline had a passion for the character Bella Swan from the Twilight movie series, her teacher developed the following scenario and Power Card (see Figure 18). Caroline then read it to the classmates in her group who modeled the appropriate behaviors. After Caroline was taught the expected behaviors, the Power Card was used as a visual support to remind her of those behavioral expectations. Data collected have revealed that, as a result of the implementation of the Power Card strategy, Caroline is now participating more successfully as a member of a group in her Spanish class.

• • •

Power Card Scenario

Bella loves being a major character in a popular movie series. She knows that to make a good movie, each character has to be able and willing to work as a participant in a group, doing his or her part to help ensure that the movie is a success. That includes arriving on the movie set prepared to work, listening to what others have to say, and respecting the ideas and opinions of others. Just like Bella, it is important for students to use appropriate behaviors in order to participate successfully in group activities at school. Bella shares the three key points in the Power Card to remember what to do when participating in a group at school.

• • •

**Power Card
Being a Participant in a
Group at School**

✔ When the teacher signals the transition to group activities, gather the materials you need and promptly join your group.

✔ Listen to what others say and wait your turn to speak.

✔ Stay focused during group time and always do your part to help the group be successful.

Figure 18. Example Power Card created for a student to help her understand and use appropriate behaviors when participating as a member of a group in classroom activities.

35

Many students have highly focused special interests. Ami Klin (2004), director of the Division of Autism and Related Developmental Disabilities in the Department of Pediatrics at Emory University, has conducted extensive research on special interests and students with autism and other disabilities. According to Klin, a special interest may bring a sense of organization in an otherwise confusing, complex world and can become a tool for understanding things. As a result, special interests have been used effectively as a tool to redirect behavior during a learner's meltdown (Attwood, 2008). For example, allowing students to focus on or engage in their special interest areas during stressful situations may help them to self-regulate anxiety and frustration (Winter-Messiers, 2014). Using special interests can also be a powerful way to motivate a student to engage in a particular behavior (Gagnon, 2006).

For students with a strong special interest in or fascination with a character such as an action figure, sports star, cartoon character, pop star, or literary character, the Power Card strategy (Gagnon, 2001) has been used successfully to teach skills related to flexibility and other challenges associated with EF deficits. A Power Card is a social narrative that capitalizes on a student's passion or special interest (Gagnon, 2001) to teach and reinforce social, academic, and behavioral skills. The strategy can be effective in a variety of situations, including when a student is confused about the requirements or rules of a situation (Kluth & Schwarz, 2008) or has difficulty with behaviors related to being flexible. As incorporating special interest areas into academic assignments can be used to motivate a student to learn new skills (Winter-Messiers, 2014), this strategy can also be an effective way to integrate students' special interest areas into the academic environment.

The Power Card strategy consists of two major components: a short scenario that describes the problem-solving process for a situation that is difficult for the student's hero, role model, or special interest and the card itself, which recaps how the student can use the same strategy to solve a similar problem (Gagnon, 2006). The card may be the size of an index card, business card, or bookmark and include an illustration of the student's special interest. The scenario and the Power Card are introduced to the student prior to implementation of the strategy, and data are collected to determine its effectiveness.

The use of the student's hero, special interest, or role model serves as a motivator and is non-threatening as the student may be more likely to do what the hero suggests. The strategy can be implemented with students of all ages in a variety of environments, including school, home, vocational, and community settings. The Power Card strategy has been used by the authors of this book to successfully motivate students to participate in an activity or complete a task as well as to encourage desired behaviors, including coping with unforeseen events, tolerating mistakes, making transitions, regulating emotions, and monitoring impulses.

. . .

Transitioning to his nighttime routine, as well as staying in his own bed for the entire night, was a challenge for Julius and his parents. What his parents expected to take about 30 minutes often took much longer as Julius cried and screamed his way through his preparing-for-bed tasks, which included brushing his teeth, listening to a story read by one of his parents, and saying goodnight as the lights were turned off in his room and his dad or mom exited his bedroom. Often, after falling asleep in his bed, he would awaken and walk into his parents' bedroom. Because he had such a difficult time transitioning back to his own bed, his parents, frustrated about their lack of sleep that was the result of attempting to get Julius back in his own bed, often let him stay in their room.

Julius has a fascination with his neighbor, Firefighter Bob. He is very interested in firefighting and tells his family and friends that he would like to be a firefighter when he grows up. Julius' parents collaborated with Firefighter Bob to develop the following scenario and Power Card (see Figure 19). As a result of the implementation of this strategy, Julius is making the transition from evening playtime to bed much more successfully, and, much to the delight of his parents, he is having more success at sleeping through the night in his own bed with his Firefighter Bob Power Card watching over him.

· · ·

Power Card Scenario

Firefighter Bob loves his job with the fire department. He knows that it is important to get a good night's sleep in his own bed to be a good leader for the other firefighters and to have the power and energy he needs to do his job well. This means that when it is time to get ready for bed, he stops what he is doing, even if it is something fun like watching a favorite television show or playing a video game, and starts his nighttime tasks. He completes these tasks, which include brushing his teeth, reading for 15 minutes, and staying in his bed after the lights are out. Just like Firefighter Bob, it is important for children to use expected behaviors during their bedtime routine. Firefighter Bob shares the five expected behaviors in the Power Card to remember what to do when getting ready for bed as well as sleeping through the night in your own bed. Firefighter Bob is proud of boys and girls who learn to get a good night's sleep in their own bed when they are young, because he knows that someday they could make terrific firefighters!

Power Card
Bedtime Routine

Firefighter Bob says . . .

- When your parents say it is time to get ready for bed, stop playing and put away your toys.

- Change into your pajamas and brush your teeth.

- Read on your bed with your dad or mom for 15 minutes.

- When your dad or mom leaves the room, say "Goodnight."

- Stay in your bed until the next morning.

Figure 19. Example Power Card created to help a student transition to his nighttime routine appropriately and sleep in his own bed throughout the night.

. . .

Making transitions was a challenge for Raymond. The teachers who supported him used a variety of tools to facilitate transitions, including, to the maximum extent possible, providing predictable routines and environments. These strategies reduced Raymond's anxiety and led to more appropriate behaviors in the classroom. However, whenever a change in schedule occurred, Raymond had a much more dramatic resistance to transitioning.

Knowing that he had a fascination with all things related to law enforcement and a special friendship with his uncle, Officer John, his teachers developed the following scenario and Power Card (see Figure 20). Data collected on the implementation of this intervention indicate that Raymond is having success in being flexible when the schedule changes.

. . .

Power Card Scenario

Officer John works for the local police department. He is usually scheduled to work on Wednesday, Thursday, and Friday nights from 6:30 p.m. until 6:30 a.m. the following morning. But sometimes, Officer John's schedule changes. He might need to work late because he is conducting an investigation or he may need to go in early to cover for another officer. Sometimes he has to appear in court on days other than the ones when he is scheduled. He may have to cancel or change his plans because his work schedule has changed; this may frustrate him, but he knows that yelling or kicking his desk would be inappropriate. When Officer John's schedule changes, he is flexible. He takes a deep breath and reminds himself that schedule changes are an inevitable part of his job as a police officer. He makes the schedule change on his calendar. When there is a change in schedule, Officer John reminds us of what it is important to do.

> **Power Card**
> **When the Schedule Changes**
>
> **Officer John says . . .**
>
> 1. Stop and take a deep breath.
>
> 2. Tell yourself, "I can be flexible!"
>
> 3. Use a sticky note to indicate the change on your visual schedule in your binder.
>
>

Figure 20. Example Power Card created to help a student demonstrate flexibility when there is a change in his schedule.

. . .

• • •

Lucas had difficulty with reciprocal interactions. Part of the problem was that his conversations tended to be one-sided, as he dominated by talking at great length about his fascination with the characters from the Transformers action figures series, particularly Optimus Prime. The speech-language pathologist who supports him at school works with him on the reciprocal rules of conversation, including the importance of shifting the topic of conversation when necessary; his peer buddies also provide support in the school environment, where structured reciprocal interaction activities are implemented throughout the day during which those conversation skills can be practiced. For the most part, Lucas is successful at generalizing these skills to other environments outside of school, but his parents reported that at family gatherings, Lucas tends to dominate the conversations with his cousins, who have pretty much heard everything there is to know about the Transformers and Optimus Prime and don't share Lucas' interest in this topic.

Lucas' parents, concerned that their son's inability to shift the focus of conversations with his cousins would preclude him from meaningful social relationships with them, collaborated with his speech-language pathologist to develop the following scenario and Power Card (see Figure 21). As a result of implementation of this strategy, Lucas is having more appropriate conversations with his cousins. Not only is he able to better recognize the signs that it is time to shift the topic of conversation when talking with others, but his parents report that he is more successful in initiating and maintaining conversations not related to his familiar topic.

• • •

Power Card Scenario

Optimus Prime knows that certain behaviors are expected when having a conversation with someone. These behaviors include not only talking about and listening to topics that he is interested in but also about topics that are of interest to the person he is talking to. He always remembers to pay attention to the body orientation and facial expression of the person he is talking to and to shift his topic of conversation if it appears that the other person is not paying attention. He knows that he needs to think about what the other person is thinking and that, if the person rolls his eyes or starts to back away, the person may think that what he is talking about is boring, so it is probably a good idea to talk about something else. Optimus Prime shares the two key points in the Power Card to remember what to do when having a conversation with someone.

> **Power Card**
> **Having a Conversation**
>
> **Optimus Prime says . . .**
>
> 1. Pay attention to the nonverbal cues that indicate if the person you are talking to is interested in what you are talking about.
>
> 2. If it appears that the other person is not interested, shift the topic of conversation to something else.
>
>

Figure 21. Example Power Card created to help a student initiate and maintain conversation using appropriate communication skills.

• • •

The Power Card strategy can also be used to support students in mastering academic content related to the Common Core State Standards (http://www.corestandards.org/) by using a passion to connect a student to standards-based content (Kluth & Schwarz, 2008).

. . .

Jeremiah loved writing and was a prolific writer when it came to assignments, but he was challenged by the mechanics of writing. Of particular concern was his difficulty with using appropriate ending punctuation. He was especially fond of exclamation points. It appeared that he created emphasis on his ideas by the force of ending punctuation (the exclamation mark) rather than by the force of his words.

Jeremiah idolized his Uncle Frank, a professor at Notre Dame University, the prestigious institution that Jeremiah was hoping to attend upon graduation from high school. Using Jeremiah's hero, one of his teachers developed the following scenario and Power Card (see Figure 22). Data collected support the efficacy of this intervention for Jeremiah, and school staff, as well as Uncle Frank, fully support Jeremiah's passion for Notre Dame and his efforts to reach his postsecondary goal of attending the university.

. . .

Power Card Scenario

Professor Frank is a popular professor at Notre Dame University. His position requires that he do a lot of writing related to his research. Sometimes when Uncle Frank is putting his thoughts down on paper, he gets excited and uses an exclamation mark at the end of sentences that do not require one. When this happens, Uncle Frank slows down, rereads his sentences, and asks himself if he is using correct ending punctuation for each sentence. He knows that to be a good writer, he has to use correct ending punctuation. Uncle Frank shares the reminders in this Power Card to ensure that correct ending punctuation is used in writing.

Power Card

Ending Punctuation

Professor Frank reminds us . . .

- Ending punctuation varies according to the type of sentence.

- Use a **period** (.) if the sentence makes a statement.

- Use a **question mark** (?) at the end of a sentence that asks a question.

- Use an **exclamation point** (!) when strong emotion is expressed in the sentence.

Figure 22. Example Power Card created for a student to help him use appropriate ending punctuation.

Make a Power Card

Function:

The function of the Power Card is to help a student gain social and behavioral understanding and to motivate the student to use appropriate related social and behavioral skills.

When/How to Use:

- Use the Power Card strategy across environments, including school, home, and vocational and community settings where there is a need for a social behavior to change. Examples include after a social "error" has occurred, prior to a transition or new experience, or as an intervention to reduce existing recurring behaviors (Wragge, 2011).

- Teach the use of the strategy by working one-on-one with the student, reading the scenario and the Power Card to or with the student, and modeling the related behaviors for him. Both adults who support the students and peers can be involved in implementing the strategy.

- Collect data to measure the effectiveness of the Power Card strategy. Depending on the behavior being targeted, use the data to determine whether the strategy is effectively increasing desired behavior or decreasing interfering behavior.

How to Make:

- Using the student's highly focused interest, hero, or role model, develop a scenario that describes the character's problem-solving process for the behavior of concern.

- Make a Power Card that summarizes how the student can use the same strategy to solve a similar problem. The card may be the size of an index card, business card, or bookmark and include an illustration of the student's special interest. Consider age-appropriate as well as developmentally appropriate language and visual supports. Using an Internet search engine such as Google Images is a quick way to find images and photographs of just about anything. Using a smartphone or camera can provide exact photos.

- Laminate the card, if possible, and place it where the student and/or those who support her have access to it (e.g., inside a homework view binder, student desk, school locker, backpack, purse; on a classroom whiteboard rail or counter at home).

SOARR (Specify, Observe, Analyze, Respond, and Reflect)

. . .

As a child, Finn investigated options for a career in the field of meteorology, and once he reached adolescence he was pretty certain that he wanted to be a weather fore-caster. He was fascinated with concepts related to weather and weather forecasting, and his IEP team encouraged his participation in the school science club. He become an active member of the club and enjoyed sharing his passion with others who were interested in meteorological events. He was also able to use this passion on a daily basis at school, where he had the job of broadcasting the weather forecast during the morning announcements.

However, Finn didn't seem to understand that talking about the latest local or in-ternational weather event was something that should take place within specific contexts – such as in science club meetings, in class discussions that focused on that topic, during his morning live weather forecast at school, and perhaps at the break-fast or dinner table at home. For example, when joining a group of classmates in the cafeteria at lunchtime, he sat down and, interrupting the conversation that was taking place about an upcoming sporting event, started talking about tornadoes and the specific types, focusing on the multiple vortex tornado and the damage it can cause. He didn't seem to understand that it was necessary to adapt his behavior to the situation – he paid no attention to what others were doing or saying, and when several students got up and left the table before finishing their lunch, he seemed to have no clue that maybe he should try to engage in their conversation or talk about something else.

Finn's instructional assistant used a narrative process called SOARR (see Figure 23) that helped Finn focus on the specific context of that situation and helped him under-stand how to adapt his behavior accordingly.

Specify	**O**bserve	**A**nalyze	**R**espond	**R**eflect
What is the specific situation?	Based on the environment, what are other students doing in this situation?	What do I need to do to fit in this context? What questions do I need to ask and answer in my head?	Based on my analysis, respond appropriately. As I am responding, pay attention to how others are responding to me.	What happened? What did I learn? What will I do differently next time?
Joining a group of classmates in the school cafeteria at lunchtime.	*Students are sitting at tables eating lunch. At the table I joined, a conversation is going on about the neighboring school football team's upcoming CIF playoff game. Students are talking about how they might be able to get a ride from their parents or take a bus to the game.*	*Students seem very excited about the upcoming game. I like eating lunch with these students, but I am not a fan of football. What is my role here and where do I fit in? I do not know much about football, but I might be able to provide a weather forecast for the game. Would students want to hear about the weather?*	*I can tell the students at the table that I am not really interested in football and that I don't plan to go to the game. I can ask if anyone would like me to check out the weather forecast for the game night. If no one is interested in hearing about the weather, I can join the conversation around the topic of the football game or I can bring up another topic (one that is unrelated to weather).*	*The students reminded me that since I provide a weather forecast daily during the morning announcements, there was no need to discuss it further at lunch. I learned that it is okay to bring up the topic of weather at lunch, but because not every student is as fascinated with the weather as I am, I need to be able to shift topics.*

Figure 23. SOARR example for a middle school student.

• • •

Expected social behaviors are dependent upon the setting in which we must function (Bellini, 2008). Many of us have the ability to approach a setting, size up what is going on, and intuitively adapt our behavior to the situation accordingly. We know when and where particular behaviors are expected and when and where they are not. We monitor and self-regulate our actions based on the context, which includes the location and the people with whom we are interacting. For example, behavior expected of adults in the educators' staff room may be quite different than expected behavior at the end-of-the year staff party at a local restaurant; behaviors expected of adults at a casual family get-together probably differ from behaviors that are expected at a formal gathering. Behavioral adaptations may require that we shift conversation topics or activities, modify our vocal volume, consider the intentions of others – in other words, that we notice, analyze, and respond to the varying dynamics of the students with whom we are interacting and perceive what others expect from us. Students with EF deficits often lack an understanding of these situational expectations, frequently violating them without being aware that they have done so.

Vermeulen (2012) suggests that social competency requires contextual sensitivity, or consciously thinking about context and which elements are useful and meaningful and using those elements. This requires spontaneous and intuitive use of relevant information even when the meaning of that information may not be obvious. Because students with EF deficits may be challenged with using context in a spontaneous and subconscious way (referred to by Vermeulen as "context blindness"), we can use a process called SOARR (Specify, Observe, Analyze, Respond, and Reflect), using a concrete situation to create a situational expectation narrative as a compensation strategy.

• • •

When Austin eats lunch at school, he walks through the cafeteria line, gets his food, and sits at an assigned table. Because students are assigned to a particular table, Austin sits with the same group of students each day. Austin likes to talk with others at his table, and he can usually adjust his vocal volume according to the noise level in the cafeteria. They might talk about the food they are eating and, if Austin notices any meat-related item that is part of anyone's lunch, he invariably attempts to lead the discussion by going into a lecture on the ill effects of meat. Most of these behaviors are typical for some teenagers within the context of the school cafeteria environment.

Austin is employed through a program that supports students in work environments. He does well at his required tasks; however, he is challenged when it comes to taking the required lunch break at work. The types of behaviors that are expected in the break room at work are quite different from those of the high school cafeteria. While some people are able to adapt to this situation by observing the setting and imitating the behavior of others, Austin has had difficulty with modifying his behavior, in particular figuring out where to sit and eat. If someone is reading on the couch he might sit next to that person and ask what he or she is reading. Also, in an almost empty break room where only two people were seated at the end of one of the long tables engaged in what might be a private conversation, Austin has been known to sit down right next to one of them and start asking about the contents of his lunchbox. In short, he doesn't seem to have an understanding of the social rules of the break room at work, in particular where to sit when he is sharing space with others.

Recognizing that Austin needed help adapting his social behavior based on the location and others in the break room at work, Austin's job coach, Eric, helped him create a situational expectation narrative using the SOARR process. (The SOARR template was used to guide the discussions.) Specifically, through the use of this compensation strategy, Austin was coached through the steps of: specify the situation/context, observe the behavior of others in the setting, analyze what behaviors to engage in to fit into this context, respond based on the analysis, and reflect on what has been learned.

To start the process Eric showed Austin the SOARR template and told him, "I'll tell you what I think about when I enter a situation like this." He encouraged Austin to visualize the situation while he modeled what might go on in his head in the context of this particular situation.

The thoughts Eric shared included the following:

Specify: *"What is the specific situation?" (eating in the lunch room with coworkers)*

Observe: *"What do I see in the lunch room?" (e.g., no empty seats, a few or many empty seats; some people sitting in groups, some sitting alone)*

Analyze: *"What are some cues that suggest that a person wants to be alone?" "How does it look when someone wants to be alone?" "Who looks like they want to be alone?" "Are there people who are welcoming?" "How do people look when they are happy to have someone join them?" "Who looks friendly and may want a companion?"*

Respond: *"I can get my lunch out of my lunchbox and take a seat where I can eat alone or near someone. I can adjust my vocal volume appropriate to the noise level in the room; if I am sitting with someone who is eating a meat-related item, it is probably not appropriate to make a comment."*

Reflect: *Based on my analysis, I ask myself, "How did that go?" "What did I learn?" "What can I do differently next time?"*

After Eric modeled for Austin how to go through the SOARR process, he asked Austin to practice how he would go into the break room setting at work and figure out how to share the space with others. He encouraged Austin to tell him what he was thinking as he practiced.

The next step was for Austin to complete the process on his own. As Austin has worked to complete this process independently, Eric has provided ongoing coaching. As Austin's skills improve – enabling him to "read the room" as he enters the break room at work – he is becoming more skillful in figuring out what the expected behaviors are in other contexts, generalizing this skill to many environments.

• • •

Timothy, a fifth-grade student with EF deficits, participates in a general education classroom for most of his school day. His general education teacher implements a project-based learning approach, and Timothy usually does well working with other students as they learn to organize their work as well as manage their time.

However, a challenge for Timothy is being able to shift from his 45-minute-per-day sessions in the learning lab, where activities are teacher-led, back to the classroom where activities are more student-centered. To encourage Timothy to make this transition independently, the educators who support him were aware that he needed help adapting his behavior based on the classroom setting. Using the SOARR template (see Figure 26), staff worked with Timothy to develop and implement a situational expectation narrative, a compensation strategy that has assisted him in making this daily transition. The discussion (see Figure 24) included the following.

Specify	**O**bserve	**A**nalyze	**R**espond	**R**eflect
What is the context?	Based on the classroom environment, what activities might occur today?	What is going on at this moment in time?	What do I need to do?	What happened? What did I learn? What will I do differently next time?
General education classroom	*Students are grouped together with their science books out. Students are either writing or talking quietly in the groups.*	*The class must be working on projects in small groups.*	*If I know which group to join, I need to do so quietly and begin working on what the rest of the group is working on. If I don't know which group to join, I should ask another student or the teacher if she is not busy.*	*Mostly it went well, although I didn't know which group to join at first. I learned that I can ask Jeremy for help in knowing which group to join. Next time I'll ask the teacher which group to join before I leave to go to the Learning Lab.*

Figure 24. SOARR example for fifth-grade student.

• • •

• • •

Jonas' family goes out to eat occasionally, but they have never taken Jonas to a restaurant that serves a buffet. They planned a trip to Las Vegas, where they intended to eat several meals in the buffet-type restaurant in the hotel where they would be staying. Concerned that he might not understand the behaviors that are expected in a buffet, Jonas' parents decided to use the SOARR process to help orient their son. They explained that this would be something new, did some preteaching by giving him a basic preview of what to expect, and told him that he needed to adapt his behavior based on what he observes in that setting. Jonas' parents worked with him to develop and implement a situational expectation narrative, a compensation strategy that has assisted him in making this new experience a successful one. As his parents coached him through this process, the discussion included the following (see Figure 25).

Specify	**O**bserve	**A**nalyze	**R**espond	**R**eflect
What is the context?	Based on the environment, what are other people doing in this situation?	What do I need to do to fit into this context?	Based on my analysis, respond appropriately.	What happened? What did I learn? What will I do differently next time?
People are eating a meal at a buffet restaurant.	*People pay for their meal first. They find an empty table and sit down. Once a waiter brings them a plate, they check out the food, taking small portions without piling the plate up. They take their plate to the table and eat their food.*	*I need to wait to start getting my food until the waiter brings a plate. I should check out the different food items to see what the choices are before I decide what to take. If there is a line of people picking out food, I need to figure out which way the line is moving and go to the end of the line. If I want seconds, I need to wait for the waiter to bring me a clean plate.*	*I figured out what I wanted to eat and got into line for those items. I noticed that some people in line take a long time to put their food on their plate; I need to wait patiently until it is my turn or get into a food line that has fewer people in it.*	*Everything went well, although I took too many desserts and couldn't eat them all. Next time, I will just take one because now I know that I can always go back for more.*

Figure 25. SOARR example for eating at a buffet restaurant.

• • •

Using SOARR to Teach Contextual Awareness

Function:

The function of SOARR is to support the student in analyzing a specific situation, assessing the expectations, and responding appropriately. The goal of the process is for the student to be able to build contextual awareness and develop metacognitive skills that will generalize to a variety of different circumstances.

When/How to Use:

- Introduce the SOARR process to the student by showing him the SOARR template and going over each prompt on the template.

- Work through each point, charting responses directly on the SOARR template.

- SOARR can be used as a preventative strategy, wherein the discussion occurs prior to an expected event or situation.

- SOARR can also be used to reflect on a situation after it has occurred.

- Collect data on the last prompt (Reflect) to determine the effectiveness of the strategy.

Specify	**O**bserve	**A**nalyze	**R**espond	**R**eflect
What is the situation/ specific context? Example: • *ordering food and eating in a restaurant* • *participating in P.E. class* • *attending worship services* • *joining a group in a general education class* • *going to the movies* • *participating as a groomsman in a wedding* • *changing clothes and showering in the locker room*	What are other people doing in this situation? How are they behaving?	What do I need to do to fit into this context? What questions do I need to ask and answer in my head? Example: • *What is the noise level/ volume?* • *Does the discussion/ tone/mood seem serious or fun?* • *Is there a leader?* • *What is my role in this group and where do I fit in?* • *If I am unsure about something, is there somebody I can approach with questions?*	Based on my analysis, respond appropriately. As I am responding, pay attention to how others are responding to me.	What happened? What did I learn? What can I do differently next time?

Figure 26. Blank SOARR template.

Leveled Emotionality

The ability to emotionally self-regulate and avoid extensive mood swings

Choice Cards

. . .

Fourteen-year-old Geraldo loves listening to loud rock-and-roll music, and his preferred place to do so is at the family computer in the kitchen. Unfortunately, his mom does not appreciate his choice of music and, when she is active in the kitchen, asks him to use headphones to listen or to change to music they both like. Geraldo refuses to do either, which typically leads to a heated verbal exchange, terminating with his computer rights being taken away for a period of time.

Frustrated with the constant struggle, Geraldo's mom decides to use a whiteboard (see Figure 27) to show her son his two choices. At the top of the board she writes, "Make a Choice." Under that, she writes on the left side, "Your music with headphones" and on the right side, "Music everyone likes on the computer speakers."

Make a Choice		
Your music with headphones	**OR**	**Music everyone likes on the computer speakers**

Figure 27. Geraldo's choices.

The first time Geraldo's mom used the board, Geraldo made an angry face, exhaled loudly, and said, "I guess I'll use the headphones." Without arguing, he put on the headphones. Geraldo's mom avoided an argument and was able to make dinner in peace.

· · ·

At times, all of us get involved in an enjoyable activity and struggle with having to stop and go on to something else. For students with EF challenges, emotional lability can exacerbate the problem, leading to an emotional outburst whenever they are required to change activities or to modify a current activity. In situations where the student has to make a change and you are concerned that she may have an outburst, consider providing a choice. "By giving their child choices and options, parents and teachers can strengthen the child's confidence that she has a role in deciding what she does, giving her a greater sense of control over her life" (Chasnoff, 2010, p. 113).

In order for choice-making to work, options have to be viable alternatives that are acceptable to the adults as well as the child. For example, 6-year-old Samantha is making a lot of noise playing in the family room while her mom is entertaining a friend. As the noise level increases, Samantha's mom gets more and more frustrated. She repeatedly asks Samantha to play quietly. Finally, at her wit's end, she yells at Samantha to go to her room. Predictably, Samantha bursts into tears, and the situation escalates.

What is the problem with this situation? It seems as though Samantha has been given the choice between playing quietly or continuing to play noisily (leading to punishment); however, there really isn't a choice for Samantha – the only viable choice is to play quietly.

Samantha's mom needs to give Samantha two options, both of which are viable. For example, she could tell Samantha that she has to choose between playing quietly in the family room and playing the noisy game in her room (see Figure 28).

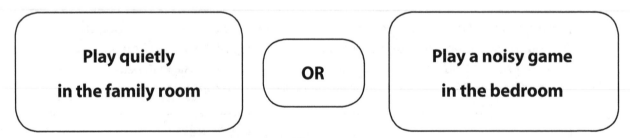

Figure 28. Example of a choice card used in a home setting.

· · ·

Nine-year old Tanner is fully included in a general education class. Tanner loves to read, but he struggles with writing. One of the requirements in the general education class is that students create book reports and share them with the class. In the past, Tanner has reacted to this requirement by throwing his book across the room and refusing to write a "stupid book report."

Tanner's teacher can provide Tanner with two choices regarding how he shares his book with the class. She decides that Tanner can either work on the computer to develop a PowerPoint or Prezi presentation or make a poster that outlines the major portions of the book (see Figure 29). Tanner is allowed to make a choice about which option he prefers.

Create a PowerPoint or Prezi presentation	**OR**	**Make a poster about the book**

Figure 29. Example of a choice card used in a school setting.

• • •

Putting the choices in writing and having the student physically choose one or the other is an effective visual support strategy that provides a concrete cue to incorporate choice-making into a student's routine (Wong et al., 2013). An easy way to do this is through the use of a whiteboard with two squares side by side. The adult can write one choice in each box and have the student put a magnet on the one that he chooses or erase the one that isn't chosen. The key is to provide the student some control over the decision so as to minimize angry outbursts.

Make a Choice Card

Function:

The function of the choice card is to provide a choice of two viable options.

When/How to Use:

- Use the choice card any time there is a possibility of an emotional outburst following a change in activity.

- Indicate the choices by pictures, icons, or words, depending on the student's age and functioning level.

- Place the choices on the card on either side of the word "or."

- Tell the student, "You need to make a choice. Do you want _____ or _____?" Point to each choice as you name it.

- Ideally, give the choice prior to any sign of an emotional outburst. However, even if the student is already becoming emotional, the choice card can reduce the level of emotionality. If the student is becoming agitated, it is very important to stay calm. Focus on the choice card and indicate, in a calm voice, what the choices are. If the student chooses something that is not on the card, say, "That is not one of the choices." Then point to the card and say, "These are your choices. Which one do you choose?"

- Use the choice card to choose between two activities (use the computer or watch a DVD), two items (the puzzle or the book), two places (McDonalds or Wendy's), or two behaviors (listen to your music with headphones or listen to music everyone enjoys on the speakers).

- Collect data on the choices that were provided, what option was selected, and the emotional state of the student. Use the data to determine whether the strategy is effectively reducing the number of angry outbursts that the student experiences.

How to Make:

- Copy the choice card template (see Figures 30, 31, or 32) on card stock.

- Cut out the choice card. If you are using pictures or icons, cut them out as well. One way to get pictures is to do an online search for images. Clipart, photos, and icons may be located and downloaded for free or for a reasonable price.

- Laminate all pieces.

- Using the "hard" side, place Velcro® pieces on the back of each picture or icon.

- Using the "soft" side, place two Velcro® pieces on the choice card.

- Tape an envelope to the back of the card to hold the pictures or icons.

- If you are using words to indicate choices, use a dry-erase marker to write on the card. Keep the marker and a small cloth eraser in the envelope.

Small Choice Card Templates:

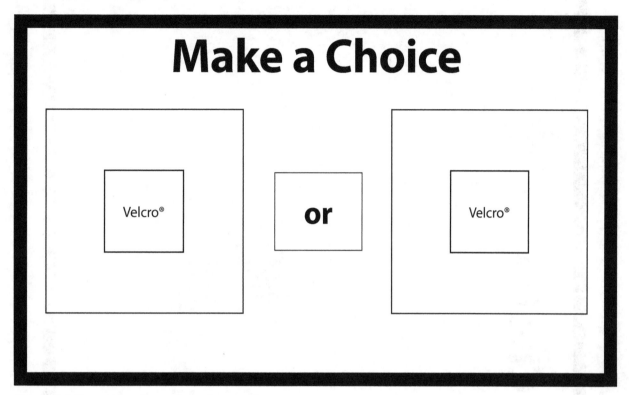

Figure 30. Example of small choice card.

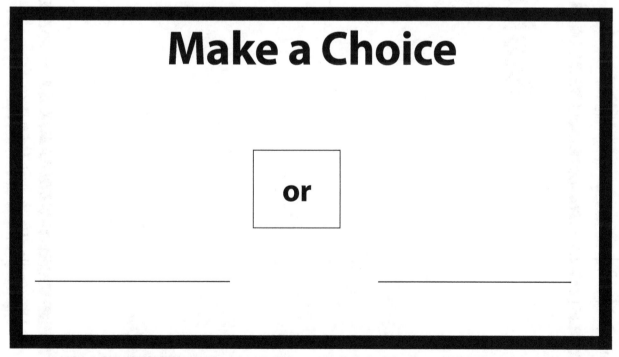

Figure 31. Example of small choice card.

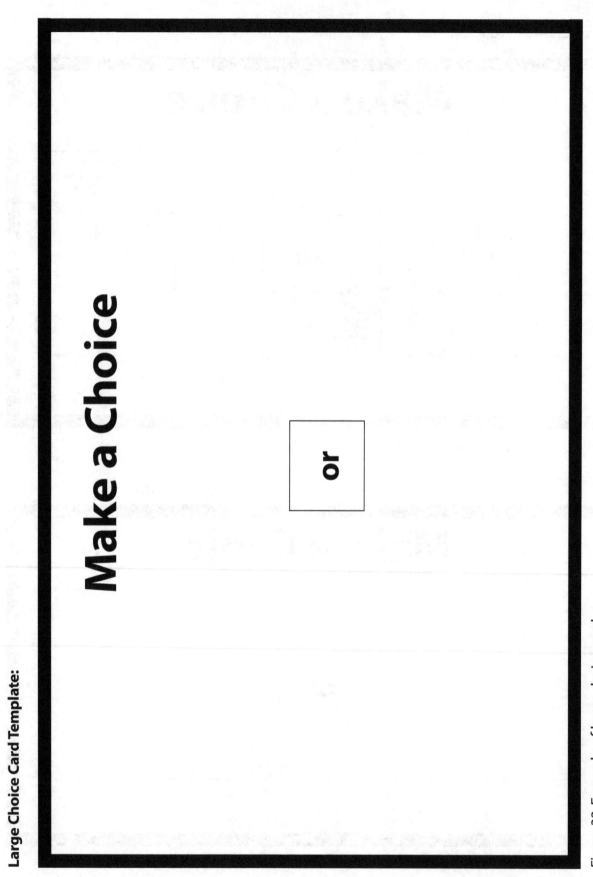

Large Choice Card Template:

Make a Choice

or

Figure 32. Example of large choice card.

Calming Routines

. . .

Sadie had a tough time this morning. She overslept because she forgot to set her alarm clock last night. Her mom had to wake her up, and she was not too happy either! Because Sadie had missed the bus, her mom had to drive her to school. Her mom was not at all happy about that either. The whole way to school Sadie's mom read her the riot act about her irresponsible behavior and the impact on her morning. At school, Sadie had to stand in line to get a late pass, and the attendance clerk reminded her that it is important to get to school on time and that, as a high school student, it is Sadie's responsibility to get herself up on time so that she can arrive at school on time. Sadie mumbled an "I know" and went to math class. Upon entering the room, she noticed that the students were working quietly on what appeared to be a worksheet. Sadie looked at the whiteboard and realized that they were working on a test – a test that she had completely forgotten about! Sadie groaned loudly and said, "You've got to be kidding me! This is the *&#%est day ever!" She then turned around, opened the door, slammed it behind her, and stormed down the hall.

. . .

Sadie's behavior, although inappropriate, can be explained as a direct response to the accumulated stress of her morning. Stress is a normal and expected part of life, and we all have days that are marked by an excess amount of challenge, which can lead to stress. However, how we react to stress can be varied, and some students with EF deficits react in excessively emotional and possibly volatile ways. In instances where the student feels she is becoming frustrated and angry as a result of external or internal forces, having a method for reducing the anger and calming down can be invaluable.

Self-calming techniques can be as simple as taking a short break or practicing breathing techniques. The challenge with incorporating self-calming techniques is that the student needs to recognize that frustration is mounting and make a decision to use the calming strategy *before* an angry outburst occurs. Using a visual support structure can serve as a cue to use a calming strategy.

When first introducing a self-calming technique, begin by prompting the student to use the strategy. Originally, the prompt might be verbal ("Sadie, it seems like you are beginning to get stressed. Perhaps you should take three deep breaths and close your eyes for a few seconds."), but the goal is to progress to a simple gesture (perhaps pointing to a visual cue), and then fading the prompt when the student is using the strategy independently. The visual prompt may still be in evidence, or it may be faded if the student becomes skillful at using the calming technique in response to the internal stimuli of feeling upset, angry, or stressed.

"I Can Calm Myself"

Function:

The function of "I Can Calm Myself" (Wilson, 2014) is to provide a specific strategy for dealing with stress or excessive emotional lability.

When/How to Use:

- Discuss the causes of stress and how both outside and inside forces can influence stress levels.

- Have the student identify what happens physically and mentally when he is feeling stressed or upset (breathing becomes more shallow and frequent, body temperature rises, hands shake, nostrils flare, etc.).

- Review the "I Can Calm Myself" template and demonstrate the movements for the student.

- Have the student practice the movements until he is able to run through them independently.

- Agree on a verbal and/or physical prompt that can be used when it appears that the student is beginning to get upset or stressed.

- Make a copy of "I Can Calm Myself" and laminate it. Put it in a place where it can be easily accessed (taped to the top of the desk, in the back of a viewfinder binder, etc.).

- When the student appears to be getting upset, use the pre-arranged verbal cue and point to the "I Can Calm Myself" template.

- Give the student time to work through the "I Can Calm Myself" sequence as many times as needed to reduce emotionality.

- Reinforce the student for using the template by thanking her for making a good choice. If you are using a specific reinforcement strategy (such as a point card), you may want to give the student a point for using the strategy, remembering to state that she is receiving the point because she used the strategy.

- As the student becomes more familiar with the sequence, stop providing a verbal prompt while continuing to use the visual prompt (pointing to the "I Can Calm Myself" template).

- Lengthen the time between the demonstration of the behavior and the delivery of the prompt, with the goal of the student independently initiating use of the template. When the student independently uses the template, reinforce her good decision-making.

- Generalize the use of the template to other environments/situations.

- Collect data to determine whether the strategy is effectively reducing the number of angry outbursts that the student experiences.

"I Can Calm Myself" Template:

Step 1: Dots **Use your thumb to press firmly around and into the palm of the hand. Count to 10. Breathe deeply. Do first one hand and then the other.**	
Step 2: Squeezies **Using your hand, firmly squeeze up the opposite forearm, upper arm, and shoulder. Breathe deeply. Switch arms.**	
Step 3: Pretzels **Clasp hands in front of chest, interlocking fingers. Shoulders should be relaxed. Cross legs. Place tongue at the roof of the mouth.**	
Step 4: Heart to Home **Lay one hand over the heart and the other over the belly. Breathe deeply 5 times. Get to a quiet, focused place in the body.**	
Step 5: Listening Ears **Gently unroll and massage both ears, beginning at the top. Massage all the way down to the bottom; repeat 5 times.**	

Figure 33. "I Can Calm Myself" template ©S'cool Moves, Inc. Used with permission.

Help and Break Cue Cards

. . .

Felicia performed well academically and socially when she was in a highly predictable environment and the expectations were clear to her. However, on occasion there was an unexpected "glitch" in Felicia's day (e.g., discovering that she has to wait longer than expected for her turn on the computer in her local library; arriving at class without the necessary textbook; her pen running out of ink in the middle of taking notes during a lecture; discovering the campus restroom she usually uses is closed for repairs; forgetting her assignment/lunch/field trip permission slip from home). Instead of asking for help, she would fall apart, shrieking "I can't do anything right!" while pulling at her hair. In some cases, she was so upset she couldn't articulate the problem.

Family members and educators who support Felicia provided a tangible symbol in the form of a folded help card (much like a table tent; see Figure 34) and taught her how to use it, thereby enabling her to indicate in an appropriate way that she needed help. By demonstrating the strategy and having Felicia practice with support, adults taught Felicia how to use the help card when needed, reinforcing this behavior as it became habitual.

Figure 34. Example of a folded help card – table-tent format.

. . .

Coping with the social and emotional demands of school is particularly challenging for a student who is easily stressed due to inflexibility, has difficulty tolerating mistakes, has poor coping strategies, and exhibits other characteristics associated with emotional lability. The frustration caused by these characteristics can manifest itself in behavioral outbursts.

When a student is experiencing a high level of discomfort or frustration, an important coping strategy is to ask for help. Asking for help is not easy for many people, especially those with EF challenges, but a visual cue may provide support by reminding the student that asking for help is a viable option. The following (see Figures 35 and 36) are examples of basic help cards that can be used to remind a student to seek help when it is needed.

Help Card Examples:

I need help

Figure 35. Example of a simple help card with icon. The Picture Communication Symbols ©1981-2005 by Mayer-Johnson LLC. All Rights Reserved Worldwide. Used with permission.

When you need help:

1. Raise your hand.

2. Wait to be called on.

Figure 36. Example of a simple help card with text only.

Taking a break is another specific strategy to help self-regulate emotional and stress levels to avoid a meltdown (Burkhartsmeyer, 2007). Taking a break can be recommended by an adult or initiated by the student, as he feels necessary. Written text and picture cue cards that are age-appropriate and portable can be used to prompt a student to take a break or for the student to initiate such a request. Figures 37 and 38 show samples of a basic break card that can operate as both a visual cue and a way of communicating the need for a break, as well as simple instructions regarding how to take a break in an acceptable manner.

Break Card Examples:

I need a break

Figure 37. Example of a simple break card using an icon. The Picture Communication Symbols ©1981-2005 by Mayer-Johnson LLC. All Rights Reserved Worldwide. Used with permission.

Figure 38. More detailed break card.

When You Need a Break:

1. Set timer for 5 minutes.

2. Step away from stressful activity.

3. Engage in relaxing activity until timer ends.

4. Return to your work area.

The idea of taking a break may be introduced to the student in a structured format, sometimes including a predetermined break area with a predetermined length of time for the break. Whether an adult prompts the student to take a break or the student identifies the need for a break herself, a range of break activities may be used. Family members, educators, and the student (whenever possible) determine what break activity will best meet the student's needs and enable her to return to work or other activities after the break.

Sample Break Activities

- Take 10 deep breaths

- Count to 20

- Review schedule or agenda for the class/day

- Move to a quiet area (of the home, classroom, gymnasium, cafeteria, multi-purpose room, etc.)

- Talk to a family member or adult staff member

- Run an errand or do a job for a family member or adult staff member

- Draw on notepad

- Listen to music

- Take a walk

- Engage in a movement activity (use a hula hoop, dance to music, carry items to another room in the home or school, wipe down kitchen counters or cafeteria tables, etc.)

- Use a "fidget" item (manipulate a piece of string or a pipe cleaner, squeeze a stress ball, etc.)

- Read a book

If you are concerned that a student will overuse a break card, you may limit the number of break cards available during a period of time. For example, the student may be provided with three break cards to be used, as needed, throughout the day. In another example, a teacher in an environmental science class provides a punch card to each student and allows students a certain number of "free" breaks per semester (Kluth, 2010).

• • •

Sonny had challenges with self-regulation in one of his high school classes. The setting was less structured than other environments on campus, and the academic expectations often led to destabilizing anxiety and stress. Sonny's teacher provided break cards and taught Sonny how to use them (see Figure 39). Sonny was able to regulate his emotions, requesting frequent breaks throughout the class period. His teacher structured the break time by limiting his breaks to four during any one class period and providing four break cards. Gradually, the need for four breaks per period was reduced as Sonny's anxiety level decreased. On some days, Sonny was able to get through the entire class period without taking a break at all from classroom activities.

Sonny also had challenges with completing homework activities. His parents found the break cards helpful at home, where they were used to allow Sonny to request structured breaks while completing homework assignments and other responsibilities.

• • •

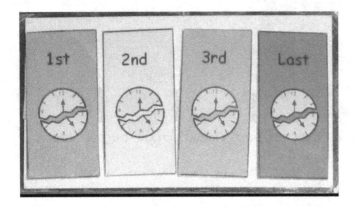

Figure 39. Breakcard used with a high school student. The Picture Communication Symbols ©1981-2005 by Mayer-Johnson LLC. All Rights Reserved Worldwide. Used with permission.

Antecedent-based intervention (ABI), as defined by Wong et al. (2013), is "an arrangement of events or circumstances that precede the occurrence of an interfering behavior designed to lead to the reduction of the behavior" (p. 20). Help and break cards may be used as an ABI procedure that includes enriching the environment to provide additional visual cues and access to additional materials or activities when a student feels overwhelmed or anxious (Gagnon, 2006).

Because help or break cards may be needed in any setting to help students modulate emotions and manage frustration, consider how the cards can be accessed. For use in the home, for example, when a child needs to request a (legitimate) break from homework activities or domestic chores, have the cards available in the areas of the house where they are needed. For use in community settings, taking into account the student's age and developmental level, the student may carry the cards in his pocket or on a key ring, or it may be more appropriate for family members to carry them. For a student who uses a master binder system at school, keeping cards within the binder is ideal.

Make Help and Break Cards

Function:

The function of the help and break cards is to support the ability to request help when needed as well as to take a break from a stressful activity.

When/How to Use:

- Provide as a visual cue to prompt the student to ask for help as well as to request a break from an activity when she is experiencing a high level of stress or anxiety. Cards may be used in home, school, and community environments and referred to if necessary. They can be placed in a student's binder, inside a school locker, etc. Cards may be carried by the students for whom they are created or by adults who support them to be presented as needed.

- Use with a system that reinforces the student for exhibiting desired behaviors. For example, when a student recognizes the need for a break and appropriately makes that request, reinforce (verbal or tangible reinforcement, such as stickers, points, tokens, punch cards, etc.) him for demonstrating expected behaviors. Remember to tell the student why he is receiving the reinforcement and thank him for appropriately asking for a break when one is needed.

- Keep in mind that the ability to request a break from activities as well as take a break can be structured by specifying break activities, setting time limits, and limiting the number of times a student can request a break within a time period.

- Collect data on the use of help or break cards. It may be helpful to note the circumstances and the emotional state of the student before and after using the card.

How to Make:

- Using a piece of cardstock, copy one of the templates or, if your "cues" are different, use a blank template and make your own adaptations. The template on page 68 is for a table tent card that is folded and can be read on both sides. This template has two cards per page and, once made, each card is folded in half. This "I Need Help" cue card can be propped on a level surface such as a student's desk, work area, etc.

- Personalize the cards by pasting in pictures, icons, or images such as those available from Microsoft Clip Art. For example, for a help card, consider inserting a photo of the adult from whom the student can request help. Add a text box and insert text, as appropriate.

- Laminate, if possible, and place the card where the student will have ready access to it (e.g., inside a student binder or on the student's desk or work area).

Help and Break Card Templates

(Figures 40-42)

I need help

Ask _____ for help

When I need help, I can:

Ask my peer buddy to help me

OR

Ask the teacher for help

I need a break

Take a break

Break Time

1. Breathe deeply 3 times.

2. Count the fingers on your right hand slowly 3 times.

3. Take a drink from your water bottle.

Blank Templates:

I Need Help

I Need Help

I Need Help

I Need Help

Chunking

. . .

Wah is excited about participating in the school science fair this year and has spent countless hours on the computer searching for ideas for his science fair project. He has a great idea, but he just can't seem to get started. Every time he looks at the requirements, he starts feeling anxious and angry. As time goes by and he continues to be stuck, his anxiety and frustration mount. Finally, he tells the teacher that he has decided that he doesn't want to participate in the science fair after all.

. . .

Students with EF deficits may not have the skills necessary to work as independently on complex tasks and long-term projects as some of their classmates. When presented with a multiple-step chore, large project, or assignment, for example, students who have difficulty leveling their emotions, or those who struggle with planning or problem solving may get overwhelmed with what to them seems an insurmountable task. Even a one-page worksheet can cause a high level of anxiety.

"Chunking" big tasks or assignments (breaking them down into smaller, more manageable parts) may prevent behavioral difficulties (Kluth, 2010) as well as help students maintain attention to complete tasks and long-term projects successfully and on time.

Before a student can break down a task or assignment into component pieces or parts, she needs to have an idea of what the completed task or project will look like. **"Getting the big picture"** or being able to imagine what a completed task or project will look like is often a challenge for students with EF deficits. It makes a huge difference when they can see what we are talking about! We can help initiate a plan by visually depicting the end result in the form of a completed example, a photograph or drawing, or a written description.

Another strategy is to teach students to **visualize** or **"look ahead"** to **"see" what a task or project would look like when completed.** Ward (2013) suggests having a student put on "future glasses" (for a young child – this could mean literally putting on a pair of silly glasses or sunglasses; for an older student, this is a figurative term) to help envision or predict what the final outcome of what they are working on should look like.

. . .

One of Kenia's expected behaviors at home was to independently set the table for dinner each night. To help her visualize what a properly set table would look like, her parents provided a template of a place setting that Kenia could refer to. Though this was a useful visual support, Kenia had difficulty completing this chore on a consistent basis. Thus, when they sat down to eat, it wasn't uncommon for a family member to discover that he or she had three knives and no other silverware, or two soup bowls and no plates. Her parents "chunked" this chore by teaching Kenia to, first, set out a placemat for each family member to help define the space for the items. Then she was taught to set out all of the plates, then all of the napkins, then all of the forks, etc. This simple breakdown of what to Kenia may have seemed like an overwhelming project enabled her to consistently complete this task independently.

· · ·

Teachers, educational staff, and parents can collaborate to support students who struggle with getting started and completing long-term academic projects. If the student gets to choose the topic for an assignment or project, one strategy might be to help structure topic choices by providing clear limits of the range of acceptable topics and/or giving three or four examples of acceptable topics. Providing a template or visual organizer to help organize content and ideas is a useful tool. For students who are unable to begin the necessary actions, help the students to activate for the task by providing a worksheet related to the project that breaks down the assignment into component tasks or parts, with a clear description of the task for each part and a due date for each part.

Once students have "chunked" a project, they also need to predict how long each component will take to complete (Winner, 2008). For students with EF deficits, if the concept of time is abstract, estimating the time needed to complete a long-term project and other tasks is a challenge (see Figure 43). As a result, they may not be able to plan for the future, and make poor choices about priorities when time is limited (e.g., play a video game instead of finishing homework).

Estimate how long it will take to:		
	Estimation	**Time**
Pick up your toys	_____	_____
Unload the dishwasher	_____	_____
Finish your homework	_____	_____

Figure 43. Time estimation worksheet sample.

Being able to manage time, which includes being aware of one's use of time and being able to manage one's schedule and tasks effectively, is an important life skill. For students who struggle with managing time, we can begin to teach time management skills by asking them to estimate how long it will take to complete a particular component task or activity. For example, ask the student how much time it will take to read the history chapter, develop an outline, define vocabulary words, study for a driver's license exam, culminate a sewing or crafting project, complete assigned chores, finish tonight's math assignment, etc. Compare the estimates to the actual passage of time that occurs to complete the activities (see Figure 44). For a student who leaves everything to the last minute, being able to estimate the time needed to complete tasks, chores, work, or school assignments within a required time frame helps a student learn to set priorities, an important step towards successful time management.

1. Estimate how long each activity or project will take. 2. After completing the task, record the actual time.		
Activity	**Estimate**	**Time**
Write thank-you notes for birthday gifts	20 min.	1.5 hours
Complete science report	3 hours	7.5 hours
Finish backyard landscaping project	5 Saturdays	2 Saturdays

Figure 44. Completed time estimation worksheet used with a high school student.

. . .

Bryan was assigned a research project in his history class that was expected to be completed over a multiple-week time frame. Bryan had a lot of questions concerning the project, and he expressed to his teacher that his anxiety level was "through the roof" as he just didn't know how he could possibly complete the expected amount of work within the assigned time frame.

His teacher was aware that Bryan would need additional supports to complete this assignment successfully. One of the first things Bryan's teacher did was to provide him with several samples of completed projects that had been submitted by

History Project			
Week	**Work to Complete**	**Est. Time**	**Due Date**
1	Finalize topic	1 hr.	5/03
2	Initial library research	2 hrs.	5/08
	General outline	1 hr.	5/10
3	Detailed research	3 hrs.	5/15
	Detailed outline	1 hr.	5/17
4	First draft	4 hrs.	5/24
5	Second draft with editing	6 hrs.	5/31
6	Final draft and proofread	3 hrs.	6/07
	Turn in project		6/14

Figure 45. Time estimates for a research project.

students in previous years to give him an idea of what his end product could look like. His teacher was also aware that Bryan had difficulty accurately sequencing and plotting the steps needed to complete long-term projects. As a result, she provided a planning chart to help him keep track of "chunks" of work and target dates (see Figure 45). This helped Bryan to organize his information, consider what he needed to accomplish on this project within the time frame, as well as other routine tasks, and set priorities.

. . .

It is not just being faced with long-term projects that results in poor coping strategies for many students. Some are paralyzed with fear when presented with even a one-page worksheet on which they are expected to identify subjects and predicates in 10 sentences. Whatever the subject area, we can reduce anxiety and frustration by **presenting one problem or question at a time.** Highlight critical information on a worksheet, such as the directions, so that the student focuses on that "chunk" of content first, thereby gaining an understanding of what is expected before starting work.

Another chunking strategy is to **provide a chunking folder** (see Figure 46). This can be a colored manila-type folder that has a series of flaps to cover content. Flaps are flipped over one flap at a time to reveal a chunk of content. The student completes a chunk of content and then turns the flap to reveal the next chunk of content. The authors have used chunking folders effectively with students in kindergarten through high school in all subject areas. It is a simple, inexpensive strategy that works well to reduce visual distractions and lower anxiety levels when students are overwhelmed by content that they are expected to complete.

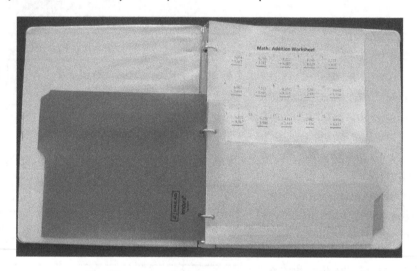

Figure 46. Example of chunking folder for assignment chunking.

We can assist students in chunking math assignments by having them **highlight the symbol** (×, ÷, +, -) in a math problem before calculating the answer. Chunking strategies for math include grouping problems by specific operation or concept or providing highlighter pens and allowing learners the opportunity to "chunk" a worksheet by operation prior to starting.

Highlighter tape (see Figure 47) is another terrific tool for chunking academic content. It can be used to highlight directions on a worksheet or to chunk math problems, as mentioned above. It can also be used to "chunk" compound words, prefixes and suffixes, root words, and spelling patterns. Content can be chunked in any curricular area by highlighting important phrases, key words, or dates. Highlighter tape is easy to apply and remove and can be reused. Also, it can be written on and comes in assorted colors and multiple sizes.

Figure 47. Highlighter tape. Images of highlighter tape provided by Lee Products Company. Used with permission.

Allowing a student to complete the first couple of steps of a new task rather than the whole assignment is a curricular modification that provides students with supports they may need to participate in learning as independently as possible (Neitzel, 2010). These chunking strategies work for home chores and vocational tasks as well. For students who are unable to cope when presented with tasks that seem too big to even attempt to start, simplifying complicated tasks by chunking them – breaking them down into smaller parts – can reduce interfering behaviors, such as a high level of anxiety, and increase engagement and on-task behavior. Pair the chunking strategy with other strategies in this book, such as a task analysis, to break down an assignment into component tasks; a visual timer to make the concept of time more concrete; a choice card to allow the learner to choose between viable options; and reinforcement for completion of each chunk of work (for example, after writing each paragraph of a multi-paragraph essay).

Social Narratives: Story Format

. . .

Each week, Marcus and his parents participate in a program at their local university that provides support for individuals with disabilities and their families. This was a positive family outing until one week when there was a change in the route they took when driving to the program. A traffic signal had been installed at one of the intersections and, as the driver (Marcus' mom or dad) approached the intersection, Marcus began to tantrum, including screaming, kicking the seat in front of him, and banging his head against the window. As the family lived in a rural area, this was Marcus' first experience with a traffic signal. His parents tried telling him what a traffic signal was used for, but Marcus' behaviors during the tantrums escalated each week, until his parents felt that it was no longer safe to take him in the car. There was no alternate route that would get the family to the program without having to go through the intersection with the traffic signal.

The parents explained their concern to one of Marcus' teachers, who offered to work with them to develop a social narrative in a story format (see Figure 48). The result of this collaboration was a social narrative written in the form of a story that included photographs of Marcus riding in the car as well as photographs of places along the route and the traffic signal indicating red, yellow, and green. The story targeted Marcus' interfering behaviors of screaming, kicking the seat in front of him, and banging his head against the window through a narrative with illustrations that defined what a traffic signal was and described expected behaviors when approaching an intersection monitored by a traffic signal. Marcus' parents read the story to him each week before leaving for the program, and, as a result of implementing this social narrative strategy, Marcus now calmly rides to the program in the back seat each week.

• • •

Traffic Signals

Sometimes I ride in the car to go some place.

On some streets, I see traffic signals.

Traffic signals help to keep the cars safe on the road.

When the light is red, that means the driver has to STOP.

When the light is green, that means the driver can GO.

When the light is yellow, it means the driver should PROCEED IF HE THINKS HE CAN DO SO SAFELY BEFORE THE LIGHT TURNS RED.

The person who is driving is controlling the car and knows what to do when the light changes.

When I ride in the car, I will try to sit quietly so that the driver can pay attention to the traffic signals.

Figure 48. Example of a social narrative: story format for a student on a family outing (text only).

Social narratives: story format are a type of narrative written to teach socially appropriate behaviors and responses. Individualized to the student's needs (Wong et al., 2013), they are useful for individuals from preschool age through adulthood. They are terrific tools to use with students who demonstrate behavioral outbursts, poor coping strategies, difficulty tolerating mistakes, as well as other excessive emotional reactions associated with emotionality.

Social narratives: story format can be developed as short stories, written from the perspective of the person for whom the intervention is being implemented, that describe social and/or emotional situations and provide a student with information about when something may occur, what might occur, when it might occur, and/or what to expect, as well as what an individual can do in a given situation (Buron & Myles, 2014). Serving as a visual cue to share accurate information, the stories may be written by parents or educators, and be personalized, taking into consideration the student's age, attention span, and level of cognition.

A variety of media formats may be used to present a social narrative: story format – typed and reproduced or handwritten on paper, as a slide show such as PowerPoint, as a book created on Shutterfly, or developed on an iPad or a smartphone.

The Social Stories™ strategy is another social narrative strategy. Developed by Carol Gray, Social Stories™ are written in a precise format and style specified by Gray. Information about this explicit format may be found at The Gray Center, http://thegraycenter.org.

· · ·

Shallanna is a 10th-grade student who earns good grades in academics but struggles with her general education P.E. class. The C's and D's she has received in P.E. have prevented her from honor roll status, and she has become very frustrated and discouraged, sometimes stating that she will never be on honor roll because she is not good at P.E. Her IEP team members collaborated to develop a story (Figure 49) to empower Shallanna and provide a means for her to overcome a complex situation.

Being Smart

My name is Shallanna. I am in the 10th grade. Each trimester my school has an honor roll. To get on the honor roll, students have to get A's and B's in all of their classes. Many students try hard to get A's and B's. Usually it is easier to get A's and B's in classes that students like. Sometimes it is harder to get A's and B's in a class that some students think is hard. Sometimes smart students get C's and D's, but they are still smart. If I get a C or a D, I am still smart. If I get a C or a D, I may talk to my teacher and ask how I can get an A or a B. My parents and teachers will still be proud of me. I will try to be proud of myself.

Figure 49. Example of a social narrative: story format for a student who had high anxiety related to honor roll status.

· · ·

• • •

Justin had difficulty during the transition to lunch. He would run from his seventh-period classroom to the cafeteria, pushing his way in front of other students. If he was not one of the first students in line, he would fall to the floor, shouting that he wouldn't get to eat if he was not at the front of the line. The following story (Figure 50) helped Justin understand what behavior was expected of him during this time of the day.

Waiting in the Lunch Line

My name is Justin.

I am in Miss Hasso's class at Traweek Junior High School.

When it is time for lunch, I walk into the cafeteria and get in line.

Some students may be ahead of me in line. They will get their food before me.

Some students may be behind me in line. I will get my food before them.

I wait my turn to get my lunch.

Standing in line helps students take turns getting their food. My turn will come. I will try to wait quietly for my turn in the lunch line.

Figure 50. Example social narrative: story format for a student in the school cafeteria.

A change in the daily routine, or sometimes just transitioning from one activity to another or from one area to another, can result in challenging behavior for Travis. Knowing that this student is more successful when he is prepped for changes in advance, the educators who support Travis were diligent about forewarning him about transitions. In addition, the following story (Figure 51) was developed for Travis, reducing his anxiety and assisting him in making necessary transitions at school.

Transitions

When I am at school, we make transitions many times during the day. We can transition from one math problem to another math problem or we can transition from math to reading. Mr. George tells us when to transition to another assignment and points to it on my schedule. Sometimes I don't want to transition to the next assignment because I haven't finished the one I am working on. It is okay if I am not finished with my assignment before I have to do another because I can finish the assignment later. Some of the other students finish their assignments later, too.

Figure 51. Example social narrative: story format for a student who had difficulty with transitions.

• • •

Jamie's parents expect her to complete hygiene habits independently. Though they meticulously analyzed the tasks necessary for Jamie to put the chain of events together in the correct sequence and taught her each step so that she could brush her teeth on her own, she continued to have difficulty. The following story (Figure 52) helped Jamie understand how important this habit is and reduced the bathroom struggles that occurred in the mornings and evenings.

Brushing My Teeth

My dentist says that brushing my teeth keeps them clean and helps to prevent cavities.

My mom tries to help me brush my teeth. It does not hurt when my mom or I brush my teeth.

When my teeth are clean, my smile looks nice.

I will try to brush my teeth at least two times a day, once in the morning and once at night.

Figure 52. Example social narrative: story format for a child with tooth brushing routine.

• • •

Make a Social Narrative: Story Format

Function:

The function of the social narrative: story format is to provide information about a situation about which a person may lack understanding, including situations that result in excessive emotional reactions, and provide a sequence or process of how to respond appropriately.

When/How to Use:

- Use the social narrative: story format strategy across environments, including school, home, and vocational and community settings where there is a need for a social behavior to change. The strategy can be especially helpful for travel, holidays, special events such as parties or weddings, transitions, and visiting unfamiliar places. Examples of when to use it include prior to a situation to facilitate social success (Buron & Myles, 2014) or as an intervention to reduce existing recurring behaviors (Wragge, 2011).

- Once the story has been developed, teach the use of the social narrative: story format by reading the story to or with the student and modeling the related behaviors. Have the story available for referencing as needed. Both adults who support the students and peers can be involved in implementing the strategy.

- Collect data to measure the effectiveness of the social narrative: story format strategy. Depending on the behavior that is being targeted, use the data to determine whether the strategy is effectively increasing desired behavior or decreasing interfering behavior.

How to Make:

- Identify a situation for intervention.

- Define the expected behavior or skill.

- Write the story. The content of the social narrative: story format may be developed in conjunction with the student or developed by a parent or educational professional.

- Consider age-appropriate as well as developmentally appropriate language and visual supports. A story written for a young child may consist of just a few sentences; for an older student, the story may be longer, as her attention dictates. Illustrations such as photographs, hand-drawn pictures, and computer-generated icons may be included to enhance understanding of the expected behaviors (Wragge, 2011).

Impulse Control
The ability to control your impulses, such as waiting to speak until called upon

Positive Behavior Interventions and Supports (PBIS)

. . .

Mikael enjoys going to recess and playing with his friends. One day he discovers that he can tease the girls in his class by throwing pebbles at them. His teacher, Mr. Hernandez, catches Mikael in the act and tells him, "No throwing rocks!" The next day Mr. Hernandez catches Mikael throwing pieces of bark from the playground area at the girls. Exasperated, he bursts out, "What did I tell you yesterday? Don't throw things at people!" The next day Mikael entertains himself by chasing the girls and stepping on their heels. When Mr. Hernandez sends Mikael to the principal's office, Mikael can't understand why he is in so much trouble. After all, he stopped throwing rocks and pieces of bark. No one ever said anything about stepping on the backs of people's shoes!

. . .

The use of positive behavior interventions and supports (PBIS) involves making changes to the environment to help students with behavior challenges be more successful at home, in school, and in the community (MacSuga & Simonsen, 2011). Briefly, PBIS is the application of behavior analysis and is focused on providing supports within natural contexts by (a) identifying three to five positively stated behavioral expectations, (b) teaching the expected behaviors explicitly and systematically, (c) developing a system for recognizing when desired behaviors have occurred, and (d) planning an appropriate response (in advance) when undesired behaviors occur (Simonsen, Fairbanks, Briesch, Myers, & Sugai, 2008). Follow these steps (see Figure 53) to incorporate PBIS strategies at home or school.

Identify 3-5 positively stated behavioral expectations.	• Consider using "Be Safe, Be Respectful, Be Responsible" as good expectations to begin with.
Identify different activities or times when behavioral challenges may occur.	• Think about an average day or week – when or where do problems happen?
Develop a matrix that describes the expected behaviors in specific contexts.	• List the specific behavioral expectations down the left side of the matrix. • List the specific contexts across the top. • Fill in the matrix by asking, for each cell, "what would this behavioral expectation specifically look like in this context?"
Identify and utilize a continuum of strategies to encourage appropriate behaviors.	• Provide the student with specific praise when the expectations are met (e.g., "I really appreciate how you were very responsible and called home to tell me you were going to be late."). • If needed, use extrinsic reinforcement to encourage appropriate behavior (see the section in this book on reinforcement systems).
Identify and utilize a continuum of strategies to discourage inappropriate behaviors.	• Provide the student with specific performance feedback (e.g.: "You were not showing respectful behavior when you called your sister stupid."). • Use strategies such as planned ignoring or timeout from reinforcement when expectations have not been met.

Figure 53. Steps for implementing PBIS at home or in school.

Build a PBIS Matrix

Function:

The function of a PBIS matrix is to define the expectations and give specific examples for different social contexts.

When/How to Use:

- Use the system on a daily basis.

- Reinforce the student for exhibiting the desired behaviors.

- Note: If you find that you are discouraging inappropriate behaviors more than you are encouraging appropriate behaviors, evaluate whether or not your reinforcement system is truly reinforcing the appropriate behaviors and, if not, make changes to make it more powerful by ensuring that the reinforcement you are using is truly desirable for the individual. Collect data on the student's response to the reinforcement and, if the response is negative or neutral, try other reinforcers until you find something that increases the positive behavior and results in decreases in the behavior that you are seeking to avoid. You may need to change reinforcers over time in order to prevent boredom and continue to elicit positive behavioral changes. Remember that reinforcement can be in the form of material items, but it can also encompass such things as attention, praise, power, privileges, and choices (Chasnoff, 2010).

How to Make:

Begin by identifying three to five positively stated behavioral expectations. Many schools and parents focus on "Be Respectful, Be Responsible, Be Safe" as their behavioral expectations. However, you may choose to be creative when developing your behavioral expectations. If you choose to create your own, here are some things to remember:

1. Choose no more than five expectations. Make sure the expectations are memorable, not just a detailed list that hangs on the wall.

2. Make sure the expectations are positively stated and actionable. For example, instead of "no fighting," try "treat others with respect."

3. Choose general expectations rather than specific ones. For example, "be responsible" invites the student to choose responsible behavior in a variety of contexts (which you will define and demonstrate) whereas "finish your chores" is very specific and only deals with a limited type of behavior and, therefore, requires you to generate a long, all-inclusive list. By keeping the expectations general in nature, you are covering a broader set of behaviors and inviting the individual to think about her appropriate behavior rather than simply complying with a list of rules.

4. Define what the behavioral expectations actually look like in different contexts. Let's say you decide to go with "Be Respectful, Be Responsible, Be Safe." Your next step is to build a matrix

that defines these three expectations within different contexts throughout the day. Within your matrix (see Figure 54; Figure 55 is provided as a template), identify the natural environments in which you want the desired behaviors to occur (in the classroom, in the hallway, getting ready for school, in the car, in the grocery store, playing with friends, etc.). List the natural environments across the top of the matrix. Next, in the left-side vertical column, list the behaviors. Finally, fill in the matrix by describing how the behavioral expectations actually look in each of the natural environments. As appropriate, enlist the student's participation in defining the expectations.

5. Teach the expectations within each natural context. This means going into the grocery store to discuss the expectations in the grocery store and into the bathroom to discuss the expectations in the bathroom. Post the expectations where everyone can see them.

	Driving in the Car	**Playing With Friends**	**At the Table**	**In the Bathroom**
Respectful	• Use inside voices • Use respectful words • Keep hands and feet to self	• Include everyone in games • Use respectful words • Take turns	• Say please and thank you • Clean up your mess	• Do your business and get back to business • Flush please • Wash and dry your hands
Responsible	• Use the bathroom before getting in the car • Keep track of your belongings and take them with you when we arrive back home	• Put away all toys • Follow rules of games	• Eat all your food • Stay seated • Do what you are asked the first time you are asked	• Clean up any messes
Safe	• Always use your seatbelt	• Look where you are going • Use toys the way they are intended to be used	• Chew thoroughly before swallowing	• Walk in the bathroom • Wash your hands when you are finished • Wipe up any water you have spilled

Figure 54. Sample matrix.

6. Monitor the student and reinforce her for following the expectations. Make sure you specifically state what she did right. For instance, instead of saying, "Good job. Here's a ticket," say, "I really like how you showed responsibility in putting away your toys today." You can incorporate a reinforcement system (see the section on reinforcement systems), but make sure always to let the student know what it is she is doing right. Likewise, when the student fails to follow the behavioral expectations, make sure to let her know what she did wrong and what she should do instead. For instance, instead of saying, "Go back to the table and clean up your mess," you could say, "I noticed you didn't clean up the mess on your table. You need to be responsible and put your trash in the trash can and your plate in the sink."

Figure 55. PBIS expectations template.

Reminder Cards

. . .

Alicia receives special education services in a general education classroom. She is successful in many areas of the school environment but has difficulty controlling her impulses and staying on task during the daily "pop-up" reading activity where the students are expected to follow along, silently reading a passage from a text while an assigned student reads the same passage out loud and then calls on someone else to read. Alicia enjoys being called upon to read out loud, but when her name is called, she often does not know where the previous reader has left off and, therefore, is not prepared to take her turn.

Interfering behaviors her teacher observes include Alicia fidgeting with items in her desk, turning the pages of the reading text back and forth, and looking out of the classroom windows. Using a 3x5" index card, her teacher makes a brief list of the class participation rules (see Figure 56) and places it on Alicia's desk during the pop-up reading activity. This Reminder Card supports Alicia in remaining focused on the reading activity. Data collected indicate a decrease of the interfering behaviors and, as a result, Alicia is more often prepared to read when called upon.

**Expected Behaviors for
Pop-Up Reading Activity**

- Open book to the beginning page (page number is listed on the board).

- Follow along as classmates read.

- Be ready to read when my name is called.

- Listen for questions to check my understanding.

Figure 56. Example reminder card to remind a student of expected behaviors for a reading activity.

. . .

Visual supports, or visual cues, are visually presented tools that enhance understanding (Buron & Myles, 2104) and prompt students about a rule, routine, or social behaviors (Smith, 2008). Reminder cards are visual cues that can be used to assist students with behaviors and daily activities in any environment – school, home, and community – and they are terrific tools to use with students who struggle with impulse control. Individualized for a specific situation, they are placed on a piece of paper, an index card, or other medium (i.e., smartphone) that is easily accessible.

• • •

Jacob is a fourth-grade student who has difficulty staying on task and completing his work at school. Completing his homework is even more challenging as he lacks the organizational skills necessary for many aspects of the task, from start to finish. Jacob's parents worked with his teachers to break down all components that are required to complete and turn in homework (starting with finding out what homework is required and bringing the necessary materials home to completing it and turning it in on time). The team's efforts resulted in Ready-Set-Go, a three-part system that clearly defines the expected behaviors in a visual format (see Figure 57) and enables Jacob to complete his homework successfully.

• • •

Ready – Do at School

☐ Write down your homework assignment in your notebook.

☐ Read over the assignment and ask your teacher to explain anything you don't understand.

☐ Put your assignment and any materials you might need (textbook, etc.) in your homework folder in your backpack.

Set – Do at Home

☐ Get your assignment and your materials out of your backpack.

☐ Complete your assignment. If anything doesn't make sense, ask someone for help.

☐ Put your completed assignment, with your name on it, in your homework folder in your backpack.

Go – Do at School

☐ Get your assignment and your materials out of your backpack.

☐ Make sure your name is on your assignment and all the pieces are together.

☐ Turn in your completed assignment, with your name on it.

Figure 57. Example of a homework reminder card.

Reminder cards should not be too detailed and must be age- and developmentally appropriate. As such, they can be effective tools for older students as they enter the world of work.

· · ·

Aaron had a job placing inventory in its proper location at an auto parts store. He was very friendly and enjoyed conversing with customers. Unfortunately, Aaron's interest in what customers were looking for sometimes interfered with his ability to get his work responsibilities carried out. Aaron's reminder card (see Figure 58), made using a business card template and kept in his wallet as a handy reminder for reviewing prior to beginning each work shift, helped him stay on task.

Aaron's Reminder Card
(Reminders for Adults Working in an Auto Parts Store)

1. Do not approach customers to ask if they need help.

2. If a customer asks you a question, answer it once and then go back to work.

3. If you do not know the answer, send the customer to the Customer Service desk. Do not follow the customer to the desk.

4. You work when you are clocked in.

5. You talk to people on break time.

Figure 58. Example of a reminder card used with a young man working at an auto parts store.

· · ·

Liam is a good student who enjoys actively participating in all class activities. He is particularly enthusiastic about class discussions, but his lack of impulse control interferes with his ability to demonstrate one of the expected behaviors during class discussions – raising his hand to answer questions posed by the teacher. When the teacher asks a question, he blurts out a response, not giving his classmates a chance to answer.

Although his teachers have defined this expected behavior and verbally reminded him, Liam continued to blurt out answers instead of raising his hand and waiting to be called on. His speech-language pathologist worked with him, helping him to understand that other students have answers too, that his teachers try to give everyone a fair chance to answer questions, and that if he doesn't get called on each time he has an answer, that is okay. The SLP then made a reminder card (see Figure 59) as a visual tool to cue Liam of the expected behavior, explaining that the card is meant to remind him of what to do during class discussions. The reminder card makes it clear what the expected behavior is – showing what Liam is to do (raise his hand to answer a question). Liam keeps the card on his desk. His teachers combine the reminder card strategy with reinforcement, and data collected indicate that the strategy has been very effective for Liam.

Figure 59. Example of a reminder card to cue a student to raise his hand to answer questions posed by the teacher in class. The Picture Communication Symbols ©1981-2005 by Mayer-Johnson LLC. All Rights Reserved Worldwide. Used with permission.

• • •

Make a Reminder Card

Function:

The function of the reminder card is to give directions to the student.

When/How to Use:

- At home, provide a reminder card as a visual cue to remind the child to complete assigned chores and/or homework, to leave the playroom/study/family room/bathroom as she found it, to press "Start" to begin the cycle on the dishwasher when fully loaded, to refrain from discussing bodily functions at the dinner table, etc. Cards can be placed in the home environment and referred to as necessary.

- In the classroom, provide a reminder card as a visual cue to remind the student to focus, pay attention, remain on task, complete work, turn in assignments, inhibit responses, raise hand to ask questions, etc. School staff may place the reminder card on the student's desk and point to it to prompt the student if needed. Cards may also be placed in the student's binder, inside her school locker, etc. Finally, teachers may use reminder cards (e.g., created on 9x11" pieces of cardstock) as visual reminders for the entire class.

- In the community, provide a reminder card as a visual cue to remind the student to follow social rules, complete expectations in the work environment, pay attention during church services, wait her turn in line, say "Thank you," etc. Cards may be carried by the students for whom they are created or by the adults who support them and presented as needed.

How to Make:

- Using a piece of cardstock, reproduce the Ready-Set-Go full-size template (see Figure 61).

- Laminate, if possible, and place the card where the student can easily access it (e.g., inside a homework view binder).

- To make additional reminder cards, determine situations at home, school, or in the community that are challenging for the student as a result of impulsivity or another behavior of concern that keeps him from participating or completing tasks independently (see examples in this section, Figure 62).

- Considering age as well as developmentally appropriate language and/or visual supports, create a card using cardstock, an index card, or a digitally created card to use on an iPad, smartphone, or other device. When possible, use language and/or illustrations that instruct the student what *to* do versus what *not* to do. The reminder card below (Figure 60) is an appropriate card for a young child; it was created on a large index card and includes a visual representation (photo, drawing, downloaded image, etc.) only (no text). Reminder cards reproduced using a business card template are especially appropriate for older students as they are not as intrusive.

Figure 60. Example of a reminder card used for a young child to remind her to use a "soft touch" when handling the class pet. The Picture Communication Symbols ©1981-2005 by Mayer-Johnson LLC. All Rights Reserved Worldwide. Used with permission.

Comments: It is important to teach the use of the reminder card by going over the stated behavior(s) on the card with the student, ensuring he understands the expectations. It may also be necessary to prompt the use of the desired behaviors, fading the prompts over time as the student independently engages in the desired behavior.

Ready – Do at School

☐ Write down your homework assignment in your notebook.

☐ Read over the assignment and ask your teacher to explain anything you don't understand.

☐ Put your assignment and any materials you might need (textbook, etc.) in your homework folder in your backpack.

Set – Do at Home

☐ Get your assignment and your materials out of your backpack.

☐ Complete your assignment. If anything doesn't make sense, ask someone for help.

☐ Put your completed assignment, with your name on it, in your homework folder in your backpack.

Go – Do at School

☐ Get your assignment and your materials out of your backpack.

☐ Make sure your name is on your assignment and all the pieces are together.

☐ Turn in your completed assignment, with your name on it.

Figure 61. Full-size Ready-Set-Go template.

Figure 62. Examples of reminder cards. The Picture Communication Symbols ©1981-2005 by Mayer-Johnson LLC. All Rights Reserved Worldwide. Used with permission.

Reinforcement Systems

• • •

Maria's teacher has been working with Maria on her behavior of running in the hall-way at school. Although Maria is reminded regularly that she has to walk in the hall-way, she often begins running before receiving the reminder to walk. Maria's teacher would like Maria to walk without being reminded, and decides to incorporate a strategy for reinforcing Maria's walking behavior. Maria is given a punch card that she can keep in her pocket; a space on the punch card is marked each time Maria walks in the hallway without needing a reminder. After 10 spaces are marked off, Maria gets to listen to a song on the computer, an activity that is very rewarding for her.

• • •

Although the goal is for students to behave appropriately without needing any kind of reward for doing so, when we are first developing behavioral skills it is important to reinforce the desired behaviors so that they become habitual. In the *Encyclopedia of Special Education: A Reference for the Education of Children, Adolescents, and Adults with Disabilities and Other Exceptional Individuals*, a reinforcer is defined as a "consequence that leads to the frequency of a behavior" (Elliott, 2007).

When a student is first learning a new behavior, reinforcement should be given every time the desired behavior occurs. In addition, when the student displays the desired behavior, make sure to tell her what she has done right (Neitzel, 2010). Simply providing a reward without specific feedback does not teach what is expected so that the behavior will be more likely to be repeated in the future (Horner & Spaulding, in press). As the behavior occurs more often, provide verbal reinforcement without tangible rewards some of the time. This will help move you toward doing away with extrinsic reinforcers (tangible rewards) and toward intrinsic reinforcers (motivation that comes from within the person).

If negative behavior continues to occur, make sure you are not inadvertently reinforcing the undesired behavior (Horner & Spaulding, in press). Although you would never knowingly reinforce a negative behavior, it is easy to do if you are not paying attention. For example, if a child screams each time her parents go to the store and the parents buy her a candy bar to keep her quiet, they are actually reinforcing her screaming behavior by rewarding her with a candy bar each time she exhibits the behavior. Instead, the parents could try using one of the tools provided in this book (for instance, a first-then board) before going to the store. If the screaming behavior occurs, they must be prepared to leave the store empty-handed. They may have to return to the store later. This will prevent reinforcing the negative behavior by paying for silence with the candy bar. In the long run, the price for that candy bar is too high to pay!

Another option is to allow the student to earn points toward a specific reward. For a reinforcement system like this to work, you need to remember a few things:

1. Identify the reward ahead of time (make sure the identified reward is actually reinforcing to the student).

2. Make the system doable (are you really going to carry a whiteboard around the grocery store?).

3. Award points for desired behavior.

4. Never take away points once they have been earned.

5. Each time you award points, let the student know why he is earning them.

Make a Reinforcement System

Function:

The function of a reinforcement system is to increase the frequency of occurrence of a desired behavior or skill (Elliott, 2007) by providing a format that will allow you to regularly reinforce the student when he makes good choices.

When/How to Use:

- At home or in the classroom, set up a system whereby the student can receive points or tokens for following the rules and making good choices. Ideas include a board with a place for stickers, a stamp card or punch card, a jar that can be gradually filled with pennies, gumballs, M&M's, etc.

- In the larger school community, plan on using something portable that either ties into the home or classroom system or that is independent of those systems. One suggestion is to put a number of silicone bracelets on your arm before leaving home or the classroom (5-10 bracelets, depending on the age of the student and the amount of time you will be away). For instance, if you are making a 30-minute trip to the grocery store with your 8-year-old, five bracelets will allow you to reinforce her appropriate behavior approximately every 6 minutes. On the other hand, if you are taking your 8-year-old to a two-hour graduation ceremony, you'll probably want to bring along 10 bracelets so that you can reinforce the positive behavior every 10-12 minutes. Each time you catch the student making a good choice or demonstrating appropriate behavior, transfer a bracelet from your arm to hers. When all the bracelets have been transferred, reinforce the student's good behavior with a preferred activity or object.

- Reduce the use of extrinsic reinforcers (snacks, a preferred activity, etc.) and concentrate on the use of intrinsic reinforcers (the joy of making good choices). You can do this by remembering to focus on why the student is getting the reinforcement and what a great feeling it is to do the right thing. It is important to understand that for some students, particularly those on the autism spectrum, social motivation may not be strong enough to reinforce desired behaviors (Siegel, 2003, cited in Aspy & Grossman, 2012). For these students, social praise must be paired repeatedly with extrinsic reinforcement, with the goal of increasing the value of social praise over time.

- Remember to **never, ever take away a token or point!** If the student is not demonstrating the appropriate behavior, he won't earn a point. However, he should never lose the points he has already earned.

How to Make a Reinforcement Punch Card:

- Consider the student's developmental level and interests when making the reinforcement punch card (see Figure 64).

- Make a copy of the "Way to Go!" punch card (see Figure 63) and print it out on cardstock.

- Each time the student makes a good choice or demonstrates the kind of behavior of which you'd like to see more, use a hole punch to punch out one section of the card. Make sure you tell him what he did right!

Figure 63. Sample reinforcement punch cards suitable for young children.

Reinforcement Card Template:

Way to Go!!

Working for: _____

Figure 64. Sample of a reinforcement punch card template.

Social Autopsy

. . .

Samuel, who is 7, is attending a birthday party for his friend Nico. Nico's parents have planned several games to entertain the children. One of the games is based on a game show theme. The children have an opportunity to take turns answering questions, winning points for their team by giving a correct answer.

Samuel, who loves game shows, struggles with waiting for his turn to shout out an answer. After each question is read aloud, Samuel jumps up and gives the answer, even when it is not his team's turn. Nico's parents remind Samuel continually to wait his turn, but he continues to yell out answers if there is more than a few seconds of silence after the question is read. Finally, Nico turns to Samuel and says, "I wish I hadn't invited you to my party. You're ruining everything!" After the party, Samuel's mom walks through the social autopsy strategy to help Samuel to understand his social error and to plan how he might behave differently in the future.

. . .

The social autopsy approach involves examining and inspecting a social error to discover the cause of the error, determine the damage, and prevent a reoccurrence. Lavoie (Bieber, 1994) developed this approach for children with learning disabilities, but social autopsies are also effective with other students struggling with impulse control because they help them to see the cause-and-effect relationship between their behavior and what happens to others with whom they are interacting. Originally designed as a verbal strategy, social autopsies have been modified by including a visual format to boost student learning (Henry & Myles, 2013).

Some students who struggle with impulse control may also experience difficulties with understanding the thoughts and feelings of others. The ability to comprehend the mental state of another person is referred to as "theory of mind" (ToM). ToM refers to the capacity to understand that other people have unique perceptions, intentions, beliefs, and feelings, and to employ this knowledge to predict how others may react (Aspy & Grossman, 2012). The relationship between EF skills and ToM is a complicated one, yet the two appear to be closely related. Some researchers feel that EF skills, specifically impulse control, are necessary for students to gain ToM (Carlson, Moses, & Breton, 2002).

Added to this difficulty is the concept of the hidden curriculum. Lavoie describes the hidden curriculum as those important unwritten and unspoken rules that most individuals understand without being taught (Bieber, 1994). Nearly every environment has its own hidden curriculum, or unwritten, unspoken rules. Even though they are typically not directly taught, these expectations are generally known by most children and adults (Buron & Myles, 2014; Myles et al., 2013; Myles & Kolar, 2013).

Think of a dentist's waiting room. Most of us realize that the appropriate behavior in the waiting room is to sit and quietly read or visit with the person in the seat next to us, and few of us would think of getting up to dance around and sing loudly. How do we know the appropriate expectations?

The interplay between poor impulse control, ToM, and the complexities of the hidden curriculum can result in situations in which students find themselves violating social norms without intentionally doing so.

The social autopsy approach is a supportive, structured, constructive strategy that provides practice, immediate feedback, and positive reinforcement, with the opportunity for the student to actively participate in the process of creating a plan to avoid making the social error in the future. When a social error occurs, typically an adult (e.g., parent, teacher, counselor, or other school staff) initiates an interaction with the student to identify the social error and discuss who or what may have caused it as well as who was affected or bothered by it. If a student recognizes that a social error has occurred but needs support in analyzing the situation, the student may initiate the discussion.

The student and the adult decide how to correct the error and make a plan clarifying what to do next time to prevent reoccurrence. The active discussion and the involvement of the student in the analysis assist him with comprehending the cause-and-effect relationship between the behavior and the consequences.

· · ·

James, a very personable teenager who struggles with impulsivity and context blindness related to ToM, is enrolled in a program that matches high school students to jobs and employers and supports the students in their work environment. James was placed in the position of returning clothing from the dressing room to the clothing racks at a local store. He was excited to start his job, and was accompanied by his job coach on his first day. As his job coach introduced him to his supervisor, James said, "Hey, Babe, you're looking good today."

Unfortunately, James lost that job before he had a chance to get started, but his job coach used the social autopsy approach to help him understand his social error and to help him in future work environments. After completing the social autopsy (see Figure 65), James and his job coach shared it with James' parents. James, his parents, and his job coach paired the social autopsy approach with the strategy of modeling and practicing how to make appropriate introductions to enhance James' social functioning.

· · ·

Social Autopsy

Name: James   **Date: November 30, 2014**
What happened? I showed up for my first day of work. My job coach met me there, and we walked to the supervisor's office. When I saw the supervisor, I thought she looked beautiful, so I wanted to compliment her like I do to my friends when they look good. After my job coach introduced me, I called the supervisor "babe" and told her she was looking good. She told me that my comment was disrespectful and not appropriate in the work place. She then told my job coach and me that I was not suitable for the job.
What was the social error? Calling the supervisor "babe" and telling her she was looking good. I learned that is not appropriate in a work environment.
Who did the social error affect or bother? Both the supervisor and me, because I lost my job.
What should be done to correct the error? I can apologize to the supervisor.
What can be done next time? Next time I can try to remember to think about my thoughts before I say them out loud. I can also try to remember that when I am talking to an adult, whether it is a supervisor, teacher, parent, or other adult, it may not be appropriate and/or respectful to use the same language and terms I use with my friends.

Figure 65. Example of a social autopsy for a high school student.

A social autopsy should not be considered punitive, and is most effective when conducted immediately following the social error. This approach can be conducted by all adults who come in contact with the student – parents and other relatives, teachers and other school staff, Scout leaders, job coaches, etc. – increasing the likelihood that the appropriate behaviors will reoccur. The template in Figure 66 may be used to guide your discussions.

Social Autopsy Template

Name:	Date:
What happened?	
What was the social error?	
Who did the social error affect or bother?	
What should be done to correct the error?	
What can be done next time?	

Figure 66. Social autopsy template.

Cognitive Scripts

. . .

Yun-seo typically ends up sitting by herself during lunch in the cafeteria, even though she would love to sit with the other girls in her class. Unfortunately, when she has tried to sit with them, she has struggled with making conversation. Yun-seo enjoys talking about science, and she often impulsively and repeatedly steers the conversation to her latest scientific interest. The other girls enjoy talking about TV shows, music, and movies, and they avoid sitting with Yun-seo because of her inability to engage in conversations in these areas.

Yun-seo's teacher, Ms. Jackson, observes the other girls at lunchtime and writes down what they talk about. She then uses the information about topics of conversation to work with Yun-seo and her mom to develop a cognitive script that spells out specific questions that Yun-seo can ask the girls about topics in which they are interested. Yun-seo practices asking the questions with her mom and her teacher, and then successfully uses the cognitive script to engage in a conversation with the girls in the cafeteria.

. . .

Many students with EF deficits have difficulty interacting appropriately with peers. Their impulsivity and relative lack of situational awareness (context blindness) can lead to frustration and anxiety, for both the student and others who are interacting with him. A cognitive script is defined as a general expectation regarding what behavior is expected in a certain situation (Volden & Johnston, 1999). For example, there is a certain expectation and understanding regarding what constitutes appropriate behavior in a high school basketball game. The behaviors that are expected and appropriate at a basketball game are quite different from those that are appropriate at a wedding.

A cognitive script is a preventive approach that provides the student with specific guidelines for learning specific behaviors (Ganz, 2007). A cognitive script can provide a visual cue for the student to inhibit impulsive behaviors and engage in appropriate target behaviors. The following scripts are for skills that parents and educators have found challenging for students with EF deficits who exhibit impulsive behaviors online and while making, or listening to, a presentation in class.

Cognitive Script for Interacting on Social Media

Function:

Social media has become a major part of our lives in the 21st century. Young people use social media such as Facebook to connect with friends, chat, and keep up with the latest news and information. Problem solving, inhibition of inappropriate behaviors, turn-taking, and pursuit of goals in an environment free of distractions are all skills required to interact effectively on social media (Ybarra & Winkielman, 2012). The attributes of the on-line environment may pose specific challenges for individuals who struggle with impulse control and other EF-related skills. First, the cognitive script for social media is undefined, with few parameters for what constitutes appropriate behavior. Second, the feedback for making a social error on-line can be delayed or non-existent. For students with EF deficits, this lack or delay of feedback may result in an absence of awareness of the effects of their behavior, or an inability to recognize that an impulsive remark or action has resulted in a problem situation. Finally, social media can be used as a weapon and a tool for bullying, especially for those who struggle with understanding the nuances of social behavior. The following cognitive script for social media can help individuals with EF deficits to navigate the world of social media more safely and respectfully. (It is deliberately stated in somewhat vague terms, to be as applicable as possible.)

When/How to Use:

- Introduce the cognitive script for social media (see Figure 67).

- Read through the script with the student and make sure that he understands all the steps.

- Have the student repeat each step with verbal prompts until he is able to repeat the steps independently.

- Monitor the student's activity on social media sites and provide specific feedback, using the card as a reference for expected online behaviors. This can be done by maintaining access to social media sites, preferably by having a copy of the student's log-on information (user name and password). Alternately, make sure that you are able to read what is posted, in order to provide feedback on alignment with expectations.

- Collect data on use of the script and effect of the use of the strategy on on-line interactions.

- Once the student can perform all steps without prompting, fade the use of the script.

	Be Kind	Be Respectful	Be Safe
On Facebook	Think about how others might feel. Only post things that are kind to others.	Only post things you would want your _____ (mom, dad, grandma, boss, teacher, etc.) to read.	Keep your personal information private. Report to an adult anything that makes you feel uncomfortable.

Figure 67. Example of a cognitive script for social media.

Cognitive Script for Presentations

Function:

The Common Core State Standards (http://www.corestandards.org/) include Speaking and Listening Standards for students of all grade levels. One component of these standards has to do with the presentation of knowledge and ideas, another focuses on responding to a speaker. Both of these skills can prove challenging for students who struggle with impulsivity and ToM. A cognitive script can support these students as they either prepare to make a presentation or to actively listen as someone else makes a presentation.

When/How to Use:

- Introduce either script (see Figures 68 and 69) to the student several weeks before she needs to exhibit the skill.

- Read through the script with the student and make sure that she understands all the steps.

- Have the student repeat each step with verbal prompts until she is able to repeat the steps independently.

- Have the student practice the skill in a small group until she is able to perform the steps without prompting.

- Once the student can perform all steps without prompting, fade the use of the script.

Making a Presentation

1. When called, go to the front of the room.
2. Stand up straight, face forward.
3. Have your hands at your sides or hold notes in front.
4. Look at the audience.
5. Speak in a clear voice.

Figure 68. Example of a cognitive script for making a presentation.

Listening to a Presentation

1. Be quiet while the speaker is speaking.
2. Look at the speaker.
3. Ask questions that apply to the topic.
4. If the speaker asks a question and you know the answer, raise your hand and, if called on, answer the question.
5. Clap at the end if others do.

Figure 69. Example of a cognitive script for listening to a presentation.

Planning/Organizing

**The ability to make plans and keep track
of time and materials so that work is finished on time**

First-Then Boards

• • •

*Savannah is an enthusiastic student and always tries to get her work done at school.
But she gets so excited that she doesn't always pay attention to the order of events
when completing her chapter reviews in science.*

*As a reminder that she must read the content in each chapter thoroughly before
attempting to answer each question, Savannah's teacher made a first-then note on a
sticky note (**first** you read the chapter, **then** you answer the questions). She puts the
note on Savannah's desk just prior to the transition to science, and Savannah now
clearly understands that the expectation is that she reads the chapter before she can
start answering the questions.*

• • •

Many students with EF challenges have trouble with planning. The first-then strategy helps
these students quickly understand the order of two activities (Kluth, 2010) by showing them
which activity they must complete before they are to start the next (e.g., **first** read, **then** sum-
marize; **first** bathroom chores, **then** kitchen chores). The strategy may also be used to show an
expectation followed by something that is preferred. For example, **first** my task, **then** your task;
first work, **then** play; **first** worksheet, **then** computer (Browning Wright, 2011). This strategy can
help a student focus on a particular activity and shift his attention to what is next.

The "first" box on the note/board may contain a photo, a picture icon, or words that show what
has to happen first. This can be a task (homework or a chore) or an experience (a visit to the doc-

tor's or dentist's office). The "then" box can represent a specific activity or an object. Once again, a photo, picture icon, or words may be used. One important thing to keep in mind when using a first-then note or board to show an expectation that is followed by a preferred activity is that the board should be presented prior to the negative behavior being exhibited to prevent the student from learning to misbehave in order to be offered a reward.   A first-then board may be used with any individual, regardless of age (Kluth, 2010).

• • •

Lamar hates going to the dentist. When he has a dentist appointment, he frustrates his parents by playing his video games, refusing to leave the game in time for the dentist appointment. The already stressful appointment becomes even more anxiety-ridden as his mom tries to convince Lamar to put away the controller and get in the car.

His mom decides to use the first-then strategy. The next time Lamar has a dentist appointment, she shows him a first-then card (see Figure 70) with a picture of the dentist, followed by a picture of the video controller. She also tells him he can play his video game as soon as they return from the dentist appointment.

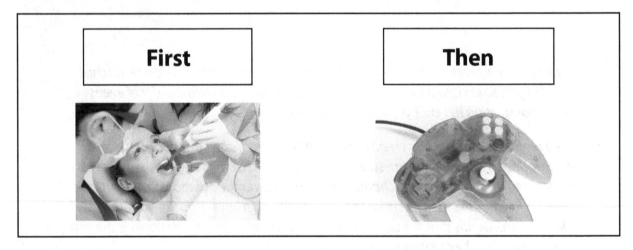

Figure 70. A first-then card used to support a student in going to the dentist.

• • •

Sahara hates math. When she knows it is time for math, she gets out her reading book, refusing to stop reading and participate in the math lesson. The teacher has to decide between allowing Sahara to read, thus not disturbing the rest of the class, and forcing her to participate in the math lesson, thus causing a disruption for everyone in the class.

He decides to try a first-then board. Prior to the beginning of the math lesson, he shows Sahara the first-then card with a picture of some numbers, followed by a picture of a book. Then he tells her that she can read her book as soon as she has completed her math work for the day.

• • •

The first-then strategy may also be helpful for a student who is struggling with anxiety due to an unanticipated event.

• • •

Aleah had a hard time when her schedule changed because an assembly was scheduled at the last minute. She was so worried about not being able to get her daily oral language (DOL) assignment done that she kept asking her teacher on the way to the assembly how she could do her work when she had to attend an assembly instead. She said she feared that when the assembly ended it would be time for math and that she wouldn't be able to do her DOL.

*The teacher assured Aleah that once they got back to class, she would allow the students to complete their DOL, even if they had to do it during what was their regularly scheduled time for math. To lessen Aleah's anxiety and enhance her understanding that she would be able to get her DOL done, the teacher also wrote a note on the way to the assembly indicating **first** assembly, **then** DOL. Reassured by this note, Aleah was able to participate in the assembly without asking any further about her DOL.*

• • •

Make a First-Then Board

Function:

The function of a first-then board is to show the order of two activities by specifying what activity must be completed first (e.g., first homework, then television; first science, then computers; first math, then reading) and what activity will follow.

When/How to Use:

- Use first-then boards with students of all ages across all environments to support academic skills, play and leisure skills, grooming, domestic chores, community activities, as well as vocational skills. The first-then board shows what needs to happen before the next activity can take place.

- Use first-then boards to support a student in getting through a non-preferred task, such as a visit to the dentist, a specific subject at school, or chores, by reinforcing completion of the non-preferred task with a preferred task.

- Use the "First" box to communicate what needs to be finished first. You may want to use a picture (a photo or clip art can work well) for a younger child, or words for an older child, or a combination of words and pictures.

- Use the "Then" box to communicate what will happen after the first activity has been completed. Again, you can use a picture or words, or both, to communicate the activity that follows the first.

- Teach the use of first-then boards with minimally invasive prompts so they do not become part of the work routine (e.g., prompt nonverbally by directing the student to visual cues and fade prompts as quickly as possible to maximize independence).

- Use a data collection system to record how the individual uses the first-then strategy.

How to Make a First-Then Board:

- Consider the student's developmental level and interests for the indicators used in a first-then board.

- Using the blank rectangles in the template, make one set of indicators to represent the task to be completed first.

- Make another set of indicators to represent the activity to take place afterwards ("then").

- Select a horizontal orientation or vertical orientation of the first-then board (see Figures 71, 72, and 73). Copy the desired template on cardstock. Cut out the template as well as words or pictures for the individual boxes.

- Laminate all pieces, if possible.

- Place a hard piece of sticky-back Velcro® on each activity piece. Place a soft piece of sticky-back Velcro® in each box of the first-then board.

Templates:

Horizontal Mini First-Then Board

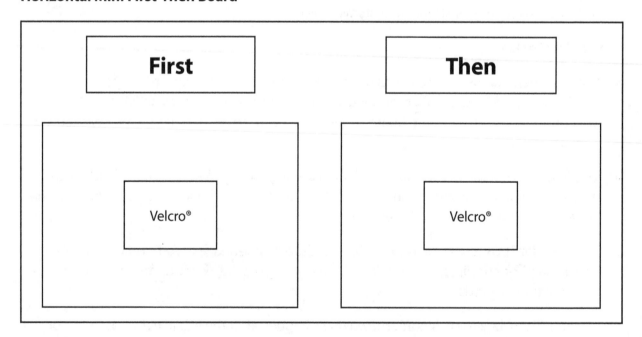

Pieces:

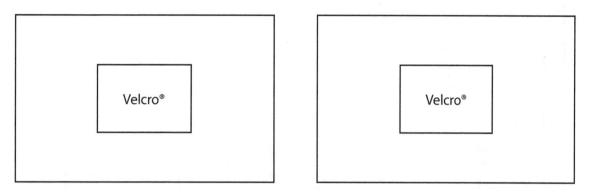

Figure 71. Horizontal mini first-then board template.

Vertical Mini First-Then Board

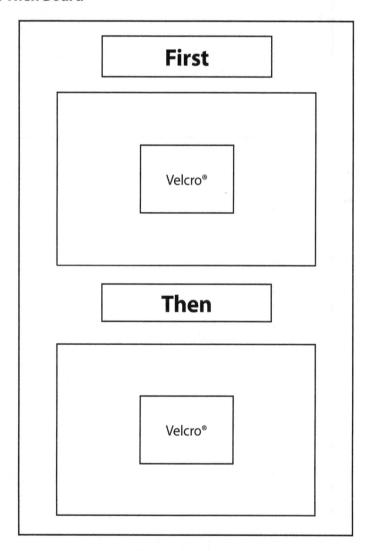

Figure 72. Vertical mini first-then board template.

Large First-Then Board

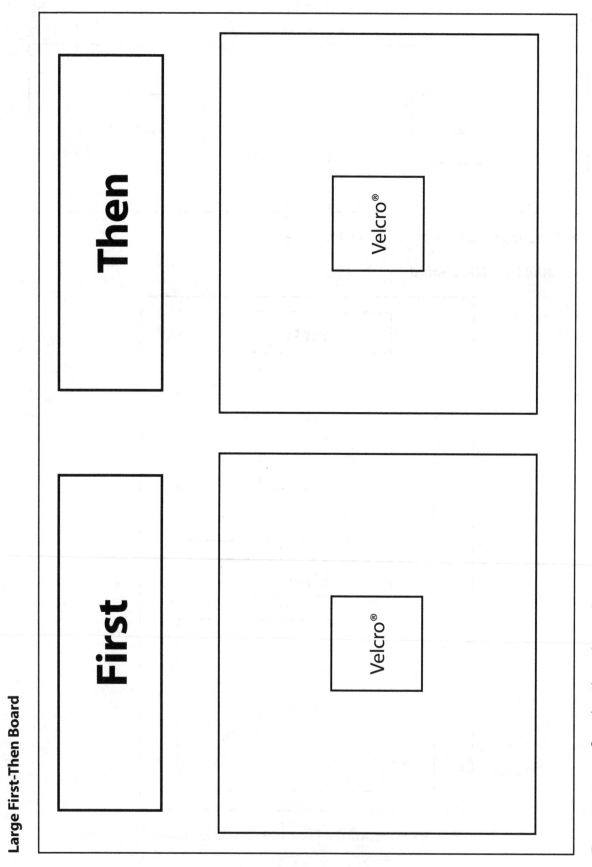

Figure 73. Large first-then board template.

Video Modeling

• • •

Misumi just got a supported employment position at a distribution center. The job site has very specific expectations regarding the process upon arrival, when taking a break, and when leaving for the day. Misumi struggled with getting the steps down and often left out important steps, resulting in loss of wages and reprimands from her supervisor.

Misumi's job coach, Juanita, decided to use video modeling to show Misumi the steps for correctly checking into, and out of, the work site. Juanita began by walking through the process herself and taking notes on the specific steps required. She also observed Misumi completing the steps and identified which ones she left out. She then used the video recording function on her cell phone to record herself going through the steps. For this task, Juanita felt point-of-view video modeling (see Figure 74) would be most effective, so she used a headband to attach her phone to her forehead for the recording process.

Juanita asked Misumi to meet her in the break room 30 minutes before her shift began. They viewed the video several times, using Juanita's laptop and headphones. Juanita then observed Misumi going through the procedure and collected data on how well she remembered and completed the steps. Misumi and Juanita continued to view the video daily and Juanita continued to collect data on Misumi's performance until Misumi was able to perform the tasks independently for three days in a row. Once Misumi was correctly implementing the required procedures independently, Juanita no longer had her view the video daily but kept it on hand to use for error correction, as needed.

• • •

For somebody who struggles with planning, video modeling can provide a visual model of the targeted skill or behavior. Figure 74 shows the four basic types of video modeling (LaCava, 2008).

Basic Video Modeling	Video Self-Modeling	Point-of-View Modeling	Video Prompting
Someone other than the student is recorded completing the target task	The student is recorded completing the target task	The behavior, skill, or task is recorded from the perspective of the student	A skill or task (e.g., loading the dishwasher) is broken into steps, and each step is recorded with pauses inserted so that the student can attempt each step before viewing subsequent steps

Figure 74. The four basic types of video modeling.

One type of video modeling that has received a lot of attention is self-modeling. Kluth (2010) describes video self-modeling as a process whereby students become the main character in the video. As they successfully perform the target behavior, they are videotaped so they can later watch the videos as models for the behavior. For some learners, viewing themselves successfully performing a desired behavior is especially motivating (LaCava, 2008).

There are two types of video self-modeling: feedforward and positive self-review (Hitchcock, Dowrick, & Prater, 2003, as cited in LaCava, 2008). In *feedforward*, the student performs the desired behavior and is video-recorded doing so. Inappropriate behaviors or errors are edited out, leaving a video featuring an exemplar of the target behavior. In *positive self-review*, the student is videotaped performing a targeted behavior, providing an example of the student's best past performance.

Regardless of the type of video modeling selected, the student can view the video once or several times, with the goal of mastering the targeted task or skill. Video modeling has effectively been used in home and school settings (Bellini & Akullian, 2007), can be used to address a broad range of needs for students of all ages (Aspy & Grossman, 2012), and is easily incorporated with the features available on the average smartphone, such as a video recorder.

Make a Video

Target the Skill	• Identify something that is important for the student to learn or do. • Define and describe the target skill so that it is observable and measurable.
Get the equipment	• Make sure that you have something with which to make the recording; this could be as simple as a smartphone camera or as complicated as a traditional video camera. • Identify how you will play back the video; will you play it back using the TV or can you play back on the device itself?
Plan for the recording	• Write a script or an outline that details exactly what you are going to say or do in the video. • Include a list of all of the steps that need to occur to complete the target skill.

Collect baseline data	• Have the student complete as much of the skill as independently as possible. • Write down what the student can already do without help. • Focus on the steps the student needs to learn.
Make the video	• Identify the type of video modeling that will work best with the student and with the task you are going to teach; will you use basic video modeling, video self-modeling, point-of-view modeling, or video prompting?
Get ready to watch	• Decide where the student will watch the video and what equipment you will use. • Think about how you will introduce the video to the student and how often he might view it.
Show the video	• Allow the student to watch the video as many times as needed before you expect him to use the skill you have targeted. • If you are using video prompting, stop the video after each step of the task and have the student perform the skill before moving to the next part of the video.
Monitor progress	• Observe the student performing the task and collect data on which steps she is able to perform independently. • Take notes about how often the student watches the video and when.
Troubleshoot	• If the student is still struggling with completing the task, don't give up! • Decide whether you need to make changes to the video or how the video is watched to help the student succeed. • Think about adding some reinforcement to support success.
Fade use of the video	• Fade use of the video by decreasing the amount of the video viewed (either delaying the start or stopping before the end). • Consider using the video only for error correction, by only showing the part of the video where errors are still occurring.

These 10 steps are adapted from the Ohio Center for Autism and Low Incidence (OCALI) Autism Internet Module on video modeling by LaCava (2008).

Organizing: Master Binder System

. . .

When his mom asked Jace if she could borrow his calculator, he told her it was in his backpack. When looking in his backpack, she found, not the calculator, but such a mess that she thought a natural disaster had occurred, including the homework assignments that Jace's math teacher stated were never turned in, the permission slip for the class field trip that was due two months ago, and a notice to parents requesting help with the school's fall festival (which took place six months ago).

Jace's teachers had shared their concerns over his organization skills, and she now recognized that it was time to intervene. Jace and the members of his IEP team implemented and monitored a master binder system that helped Jace organize his assignments and keep track of paperwork.

. . .

Many students have trouble organizing what they need to bring from school to home and back to school. Visual supports include any tool presented visually that supports an individual as he moves through his day (Smith, 2008). A master binder system is a type of visual support that may help students be more successful in planning and organization and, therefore, help better fulfill their academic responsibilities both at home and at school. Some schools teach this type of system starting in kindergarten, where young learners develop good organizational habits. Such habits are especially important in middle school and high school, where some of the demands on EF skills include multiple assignments and teachers, a fast-moving schedule, rapidly increasing expectations, and a limited time frame for homework and community and home activities.

No one system for keeping paperwork organized is appropriate for all students. Understanding your student's organizational issues will help you determine what strategies will be effective. Some schools or teachers have specific rules about binders, so accommodations may be necessary to meet the needs of individual students. Schools may supply binders or may recommend a type that has worked well with other students. This might be a three-ring binder with sections organized by subject. Depending on the student's grade level, it may include "To Do" lists, a daily schedule as well as a long-range planning calendar, a homework reminder card, and a place to record homework assignments (Bloomfield, 2009).

Using a master binder system enables students to store and retrieve homework, assignments, and other papers in an organized way, thereby helping them manage time, materials, and activities. It also helps parents stay informed and connected about homework, classroom policies, and special events or projects. Instructions for how to make a master binder system are included in this section.

Electronic organization may be a good option for students who have difficulties with the fine-motor skills necessary for writing down homework assignments. Recording assignments, tasks, and reminders on a recording device may be considered; a quick response (QR) code for the assignments of the day may be posted on the teacher's classroom door for students to scan with a smartphone. And a student who has difficulty getting assignments back and forth between school and home might email assignments from home to himself or directly to the teacher.

Make a Master Binder System

Function:

The function of a master binder system is to help students organize and keep track of schoolwork and other important information so that work is finished on time.

When/How to Use:

- Make sure the system is used on a daily basis. Teach the student how to use the system (review agenda for each day, record homework assignments, look at due dates for long-term assignments and estimate time needed to complete work, store and retrieve paperwork effectively, maintain system by reviewing once a week, etc.).

- Work with parents to help the student by creating a routine that ensures that his binder is placed in his backpack before he leaves for school each day and returned to his backpack at the end of the day.

- Support the system by establishing a time to check and assist the student in organizing the binder. Depending on the student's needs, check-in may be weekly, daily, or several times throughout the day. This is a good time to check that notes are in the right place, loose papers are placed in the sections to which they belong, and outdated documents are removed. Once the student has mastered the skill of keeping his binder organized, conducting spot checks is a good idea to ensure the student continues to use the system successfully (Duncan, Rock, & Szakacs, 2010). Combine with other strategies outlined in this book, such as video modeling and reinforcement.

- Use a data collection system to record how the student uses and maintains the master binder system.

Recommended Materials:

- *An appropriate binder.* A sturdy three-ring style is a good choice. For a younger elementary grade-level student, a binder with ½-inch rings may be the proper size for holding all necessary paperwork; for students in the upper grades, including middle and high school, a 2- to 3-inch binder may be needed to store all materials.

- *Student day planner.* This may be purchased or created and downloaded (e.g., using calendaring software such as Microsoft Outlook). It should include a monthly calendar for recording long-term assignments and noting upcoming school activities as well as a daily calendar for documenting daily assignments (some calendaring systems may be set up in the planner by week; that is fine as long as it includes plenty of room to record daily events by the day – most important, homework assignments). Use of a planner to map out assignments for the day *and* over time is essential for being able to apply the concept of organization (Winner, 2000).

- *Any pertinent information specific to the student's school* (school bell schedule, a map of the school, student behavior expectations, dress codes, etc.). This type of information is usually sent home with students at the beginning of the school year.

- *Subject dividers.* Determine how many dividers are needed to break down the binder contents by section (e.g., how many subjects/classes does the student have? You might want one section per subject plus sections for information specific to the school as described above).

- *Sheet protectors* for holding frequently referenced documents for each subject (numbers vary depending on the needs of the student).

- *A two-pocket folder for each class.* Consider color-coding – use a different-colored folder for each subject, and highlight the matching subject with the same color on the bell schedule. Covering textbooks by subject in corresponding colored paper helps learners with organizational deficits easily refer to necessary materials when needed ("red" = math; "green" = language arts, etc.).

- *Two sticky-back labels for each folder.*

- *An accessory bag* (such as a clear pencil pouch) to hold items such as pencils, pens, small sticky notes, highlighter pens and/or tape, and a three-hole punch. Also include visual supports, such as those described in this book, including a Ready-Set-Go homework reminder card (impulse control), help and/or break cards (leveled emotionality), and wait card, countdown timer, and visual scale from the section on flexibility.

- *Notebook paper.*

How to Make:

- Determine how many dividers are needed to break down the binder contents by section. You might want one section per subject plus sections for the school bell schedule, a map of the school, and information specific to the school – student behavior expectations, dress codes, etc.

- Label a subject on each divider for each class, as well as any other sections described above.

- Place dividers in the binder, arranging dividers for subjects in chronological order according to daily schedule.

- Place sheet protectors behind dividers.

- Select a pocket folder for each subject. Using sticky-back labels, label the left pocket inside each pocket folder "Homework and Paperwork **to Take Home**." Label the right pocket inside each pocket folder "Homework and Paperwork **to Be Returned to School**." Place one two-pocket folder behind the divider for each subject. Clearly identify where homework, completed assignments, and handouts should be placed (National Education Association, 2006).

- Add notebook paper – 25 pages in each section for note taking is a good start.

- Insert accessory bag into the binder in front of all other contents.

- Help the student organize papers by subject and insert any pertinent school information.

There is no "one-size-fits-all" approach to creating and using a master binder system. What is an appropriate system for a kindergarten student (the binder may not need to include sections divided by subject; it may be as simple as a narrow binder containing pertinent school information – calendar, behavioral expectations, etc., as well as one portfolio for paperwork that goes back and forth from school to home) is very different from what is appropriate for an older student who has multiple teachers in multiple locations across campus. Different systems work for different students. The important thing is that the student learns a system that is easy to use and lets her organize, store, and retrieve paperwork on time.

Contingency Mapping

. . .

Kai's teacher, Ms. McDonald, is incorporating more group work into her social studies lessons this year. Although most of the students seem to enjoy working in groups, Kai prefers to work alone and refuses to work with his group. Ms. McDonald has tried to explain to Kai that it is important for him to learn to work with others, but Kai flatly refuses to do so. When it is time for group work, Kai takes out his book and sits at his desk, while his group works at a table nearby.

Ms. McDonald decides to implement a strategy recommended by the school psychologist. She develops a contingency map (see Figure 75).

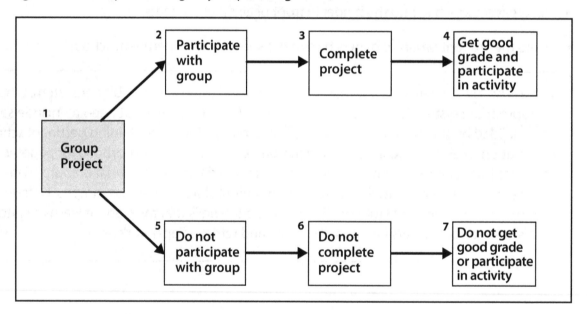

Figure 75. Contingency map for Kai.

The map shows that Kai can choose to participate with his group, which will allow him to complete the group project, leading to a good grade on the project and an opportunity to participate in the monthly social studies activity, which includes a guest speaker and a video, which Kai enjoys immensely. On the other hand, Kai can choose not to participate with his group, which means he will not complete the group project, leading to an inability to receive the grade for the project or participate in the activity.

Based on the contingency map, Kai decides to participate with his group so that he can finish the project, get a good grade, and participate in the final activity. He finds that working in a group is less difficult than he thought it would be, and chooses to participate in group projects in the future without making a fuss.

. . .

Applied behavior analysis (ABA) is based upon the tenet that all behavior serves a specific function for the person displaying a given behavior. At its most basic level, human beings behave in a specific way either to get something (attention, a preferred activity or object, a sensory need) or to avoid something (attention, a non-preferred activity or object, sensory stimulation). Behaviorists often use a technique called functional equivalence training, or FET, to teach alternative replacement behaviors that take the place of the problem behavior (Sprague & Horner, 1999). Typically, FET is paired with prompting/fading and reinforcement to encourage the student to perform the desired behavior. However, when reinforcement alone does not work to change the behavior, a technique called contingency mapping (CM) may be used to encourage the student to choose the desired behavior over the problem behavior (Brown & Mirenda, 2011).

Contingency mapping is a type of visual support that can be used to support FET. Contingency maps use visual representations designed to demonstrate the relationship between what happens prior to a behavior (antecedent) occurring and what the results of the behavior might be (consequence). In order to be effective, a contingency map must show the following components and the relationships between them.

1. *The antecedent*, or what happens prior to the behavior. For example, the antecedent for Kai's behavior is the direction by Ms. McDonald for students to work in groups.

2. *The actual behavior* (the problem behavior and the functional equivalent, or desired behavior). In Kai's example, the problem behavior is his refusal to participate with the group and his choice to read his book alone. The desired behavior is for him to participate in the group.

3. *The reinforcer that will be made available* upon the occurrence of the desired behavior. The reinforcer used with Kai is the grade he will earn for completing the group project, as well as participation in the class activity.

4. *The reinforcer that will no longer be made available* following the occurrence of the problem behavior. The reinforcer that will no longer be made available when Kai chooses not to participate in group work is the grade and the participation in the class activity.

Contingency mapping can be used to help students with EF deficits to understand the effects of their behavioral choices. As such, CM can provide a way of communicating how choices can affect our lives and can support us in seeing "down the road" and, thus, making a better choice in the immediate future.

• • •

> *Jesse often leaves the dinner table without clearing his plate and utensils, despite being asked by his parents repeatedly to do so. His parents observe Jesse's behavior and discuss possible functions of his behavior. In particular, they notice that he leaves the table quickly after dinner and rushes off to the computer to play his favorite video game. Thus, they hypothesize that the function of Jesse's behavior is to get access to*

the computer and the computer game. Because Jesse enjoys playing his computer game, his parents decide to make playing the computer game contingent upon him clearing his plate and utensils. They develop the following CM (Figure 76) to illustrate the behavioral choices and the consequences of each for Jesse.

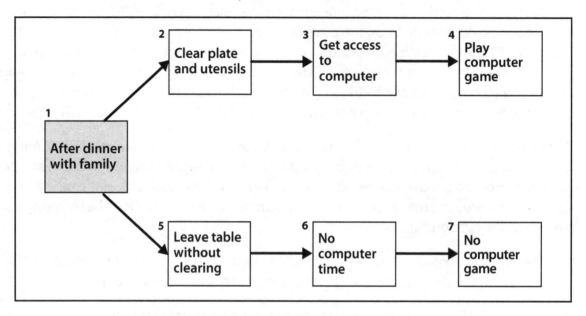

Figure 76. Example of a contingency map used in a home situation.

• • •

Make a Contingency Map

Function:

The function of a contingency map is to provide a format that will allow the student to visualize the effects of her choices.

When/How to Use:

- Identify the target behavior that is causing difficulties and analyze the function of the behavior.

- If needed, set up a system whereby the student can receive points or tokens for following the rules and making good choices (see the section on reinforcement systems for ideas). In some cases, completion of the desired behavior will naturally result in reinforcement (e.g., when Kai participated with his group and finished the assignment, he received a grade for the group project). In other cases, it may be necessary to develop the reinforcement system before the contingency map and incorporate the reinforcement. For example, Jesse's parents may decide to incorporate a system whereby Jesse receives points for clearing his plate and utensils, allowing him to use his accumulated points to access the computer at the end of the week, instead of allowing computer time each day.

- Decide what the consequences of the behavior (both desired and problem) are.

- Fill out the CM, including the antecedent in the far-left box, the behaviors in the first two boxes to the right, and the consequences to the right of the behavior. Decide whether you need to include both pictures and words or if words are sufficient (based on the needs of the individual child).

- Remember that the consequence of choosing the undesired behavior is not punishment! Instead, it is lack of access to the reinforcement.

- Review the CM with the student to ensure that he understands how his behavior relates to the antecedent and how the consequences of the behavior are related to the behavior that is selected.

- As the student selects a certain behavior, review the CM with him and discuss how the consequences (positive or negative) relate to the selected behavior.

- As the student consistently selects the functionally equivalent (desired) behavior, first fade the use of the CM and then fade the use of the selected reinforcer.

How to Make a Contingency Map:

- Consider the student's developmental level and interests.

- Make a copy of the CM template (see Figure 77) and print it out.

- Fill in the blanks on the CM, following these guidelines:

  1. The antecedent (what will happen first)

  2. The desired behavior

  3. The effects of the desired behavior

  4. The reinforcement received

  5. The undesired behavior

  6. The effects of the undesired behavior

  7. The reinforcement that will not be received

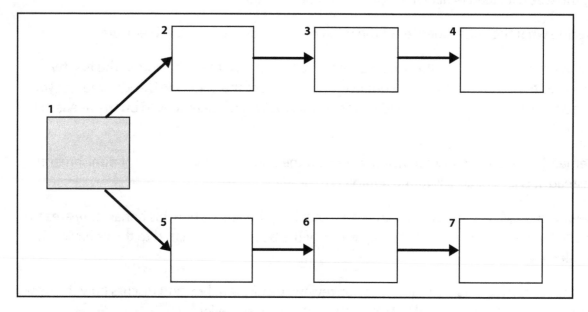

Figure 77. Contingency map template.

Project Mapping

. . .

Kehinde is in the 12th grade at a charter school. Twelfth-grade students at the school prepare a senior project that is presented to parents, students, and community members at the end of the school year. Students work on the project throughout the year, and the presentations at the end of the year are a very big deal. Kehinde is excited about the senior project but a little worried about organizing her time so that she can get everything done. She knows that one strategy for keeping things straight is to make notes regarding what has to be done in order for the project to be completed. She has been making notes on sticky notes and stuck them on everything, from her bathroom mirror to the covers of her schoolbooks. But seeing the myriad sticky notes is not lessening Kehinde's sense of being overwhelmed. She needs a way to organize her notes into a system that will help her to know what she needs to do, when to do it, and what steps she has already completed.

. . .

Many students with EF deficits struggle with planning to complete a long-term project. For older students, long-term assignments can be especially challenging because planning, prioritizing, and recognizing the length of project sections may all be areas of weakness (Constable, Grossi, Moniz, & Ryan, 2013). Understanding the discrete parts required for a long-term project, underestimating the amount of time needed to complete each part, failing to complete each section in a timely manner, and leaving too much to be done at the last minute can all contribute to an end product that is, well, not ready in the end!

Project mapping is a strategy that allows the student to visualize the discrete parts of an assignment, put a time frame on each part, plan when the parts need to be completed in order to be able to finish the project, and monitor progress toward completion of the project. Use of this strategy allows the student to work backwards from the actual due date and is flexible enough to be used with both simple and very complex projects.

See Figure 78 for an example of a project map developed for a student working on a research paper that requires several linked steps.

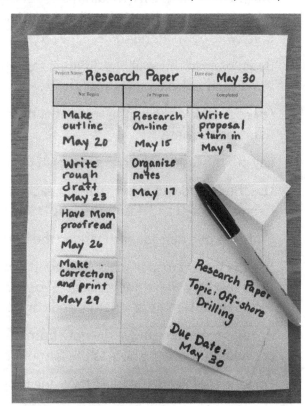

Figure 78. Project map example.

Map out a Project

Function:

The function of a project map is to provide a system that allows the student to identify the different parts of a project and organize them in such a way as to visualize the time frame and order in which the parts need to be completed to ensure timely completion of the project.

Materials Needed:

- Sticky notes (small and medium sizes – assorted colors)

- Calendar

- Project map planner

When/How to Use:

- Use the project map any time students have an assignment due that consists of more than three discrete parts that need to be completed and when the due date is one or more weeks into the future.

- Begin by identifying what the finished product will look like. Will it be a written report or an oral presentation? On a medium-sized sticky note, ask the student to write down the basic information regarding the project, including format and topic. *At the bottom of the sticky note, write down the due date of the project.*

- Begin brainstorming all the different tasks that need to be completed to finish the project. Write each task on a small sticky note.

- For each task, estimate the amount of time it will take to complete. Write this under the task name on the note.

- Lay out the tasks in the order in which they should be completed.

- Use the calendar to assign dates to each task, giving each task the amount of time that has been estimated and ensuring that all tasks will be finished before the final due date.

- Write the due date for each task on the bottom of the sticky note.

- Use the project map planner (see sample in Figure 79) to place the sticky note tasks in order. Place tasks that have not yet been begun in the "Not Begun" column, tasks that are in progress in the "In Progress" column, and completed tasks in the "Completed" column.

- As tasks are begun, move the note from the left column to the middle column. As a task is completed, move the note to the far-right column.

- For longer projects, use more than one project map planner.

- Use a data collection system to record how the individual uses the project mapping strategy.

Project Map Planner:

Project Name:		Date Due:
Not Begun	In Progress	Completed

Figure 79. Project map planner.

Comment: To adapt the project mapping strategy for use with a group project, develop the project map as indicated, using different-colored sticky notes for different members of the group. Place the project map where all members of the group can see it and monitor progress toward completion.

Problem Solving

The ability to know when there is a problem that needs to be solved, generate solutions, select one, and evaluate the outcome

Work Systems

• • •

Jarrod followed his individual visual schedule, but once he arrived at the location where he was expected to work independently, often he couldn't seem to get started on the assigned tasks. And even if he was able to get started, on many occasions he needed frequent adult support. "How much work do I have to do," "How much time will it take?," How long will I be here?," and "What do I do when I'm finished?" were questions that he commonly asked.

Understanding that Jarrod was highly motivated to go to the Lego® table when his work was completed but that he lacked the problem-solving skills necessary to figure out what he had to do during his independent work time, Jarrod's IEP team developed and implemented a matching work system. The system includes information Jarrod needs about the process of working on tasks during his independent work time. Jarrod is highly motivated to use his work system as he can clearly see what work he has to do, and he is motivated to finish his work because he gets to go to the Lego® table after completing the activities listed in his work system. Finally, data indicate that, as a result of implementing a work system, Jarrod is able to work independently and the need for adult intervention when using the work system has been greatly reduced.

• • •

A work system is an organized presentation of tasks and materials that teaches a student how to work efficiently and independently. As such, work systems help a student who has difficulty initiating tasks by organizing tasks to show how much work she has to do and reduce anxiety for a student who needs to have a clear understanding of when she will be finished (Hume & Odom, 2007). A work system can support problem solving in individuals with EF deficits by supporting self-determination through increasing independence and lessening the reliance on direction from adults. Teaching students to be self-regulated problem-solvers builds skills that can support independence in different settings throughout the lifespan (Palmer & Wehmeyer, 2003).

Work systems are an environmental modification that provides structure for students who struggle with executive function. As such, they are an important compensation strategy that can support many of the components of executive function, including flexibility, leveled emotions, planning, and problem solving.

Work systems motivate students to get started and reach the "finished" point because they can clearly see "start" and "finish." It is a routine that builds flexibility – the activities may change, but the system for completing the work remains the same.

Work systems, which are effective in school, home, and vocational environments, can be developed to break a task into small steps that create an "action plan" or to represent a set of tasks or jobs that a student will complete during a specific amount of time and will answer the following four questions (Mesibov, Shea, & Schopler, 2005):

1. **What work do I have to do?** Information in a work system is visually presented at a level that is understandable to the student (Hume, 2010) using words, numbers, and/or icons that express the number of tasks to be completed as well as what the student will "earn" or is expected to do upon completion, or what task or activity is next. In a matching work system, students match symbols to corresponding tasks that they complete independently. For example, Jarrod used a daily visual schedule (see Figure 80) that represented all of his morning school activities, including his "Independent Work." His matching work system (see Figure 81) showed what work he was expected to complete during his independent work time. A matching work system can have a left-to-right or a top-to bottom orientation.

Jarrod's Morning Schedule
Writer's Workshop
Reading
Recess
Math
Independent Work
Lunch

Figure 80. Jarrod's individual visual schedule.

Figure 81. Jarrod's matching work system for "Independent Work" using a left-to-right orientation. The Picture Communication Symbols ©1981-2005 by Mayer-Johnson LLC. All Rights Reserved Worldwide. Used with permission.

2. **How much work do I have to do?** The task materials are organized and counted out ahead of time so that the student can clearly see what he is going to do (Mesibov & Shea, 2014). For example, the student may start with five tasks to be completed in a 15-minute work period. Each task is represented by an indicator – picture, symbol, or number – that the student removes and matches to the individual tasks (see Figure 82). As the student completes each task, he pulls the next number (which indicates which task to match it to) to find the next task. This is a concrete representation of "how much work."

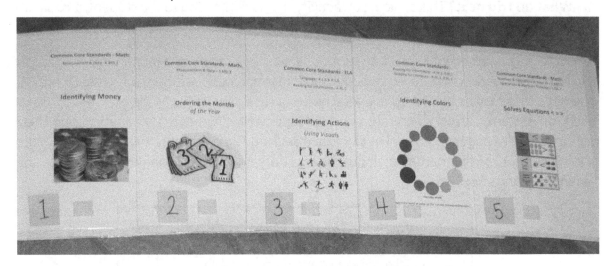

Figure 82. Jarrod's tasks, labeled with numbers as indicators for matching.

Figure 83. Jarrod matching first indicator (the numeral "1") to the first task. The Picture Communication Symbols ©1981-2005 by Mayer-Johnson LLC. All Rights Reserved Worldwide. Used with permission.

3. **How do I know when my work is finished?** For example, the matching work system (see Figure 83) includes numbers from 1-5 and a symbol, using words, pictures, or icons that represent what happens once the student completes all five tasks. What happens next could be an activity that is reinforcing to a student (for many students, this is often a motivation to complete all tasks). After all five numbers have been pulled and all tasks are completed, the student can see that all of the work has been finished.

4. **What do I do next?** This could be an activity that is reinforcing to the student; it could also simply be what is next on the student's schedule of activities.

Any task can be turned into a work system. For example, a recipe or directions for making coffee can become a work system for somebody who is learning basic self-help skills (see Figure 84). The directions may be laminated and attached to a clipboard with a "wipe-off" pen for repeated use. Work systems can also be created for academic or employment-related tasks using check-off systems with paper and pencil or electronic devices. The concept remains the same in giving the individual explicit information about the amount of work to be done and what comes next when the work is finished.

Work System for Making Coffee

- Take coffee pot and place on table.

- Open filter basket.

- Put paper filter into filter basket.

- Close filter basket.

- Pour water from pitcher into glass coffee pot.

- Pour water from coffee pot into coffee well.

- Close coffee well.

- Plug in coffee pot.

- Turn on (see happy face sticker).

- Put supplies away.

- Check your schedule for next activity.

Figure 84. Example of a written list work system.

Make a Work System

Function:

The function of a work system is to communicate the expectations for a set of tasks or jobs the student will complete independently during a specified length of time. A work system can increase independence and lessen reliance on adults.

When/How to Use:

- Use work systems with students of all ages across all environments to support academic skills, play and leisure skills, grooming, domestic chores, community activities, as well as vocational skills. The tasks that students are expected to complete are activities and skills that have been previously mastered (Carnahan, 2008). Work systems communicate what work the student has to do, how much work he or she has to do, how she will know when she is finished, and what happens next.

- Individualize work systems, taking into account a student's strengths and interests. With a matching work system, tasks or steps may be visually represented by pictures, symbols, words, icons, or other indicators corresponding to the tasks/activities to be completed. A matching indicator is attached in left-to-right or top-to-bottom progression on a matching work system strip. An additional matching set of indicators may also be created to attach to the tasks the student is to complete (see Figure 85). In this case, the student matches the indicator to the corresponding task and completes the task or activity represented by the indicator.

Figure 85. Example of matching work system with capital letters A, B, and C as indicators for three tasks. A matching set of indicators below the work system strip labels corresponding tasks A, B, and C. "What do I do next?" for this student is to transition to the art center.

- Continue the progression left to right or top to bottom until all tags/indicators are matched and all tasks have been completed.

- Be sure to visually indicate what the student is to do once she has completed the activities on the matching work system. You may need to use a highly desired item or activity to increase motivation; however, often being "finished" is motivating enough. For example, after completing domestic chores, the student may be provided the opportunity to listen to music; after completing academic tasks at school, the student might have the opportunity to read his book of choice. The "What's next?" could also be a cue to "Check your schedule" to see what the student is expected to do after completing all activities/tasks within the work system.

- Teach the work system with minimally invasive prompts so the adult prompts do not become part of the work routine (e.g., prompt nonverbally by directing the student to visual cues and fade prompts as quickly as possible to maximize independence).

- Use a data collection system to record student behavior during independent work time.

How to Make a Matching Work System:

- Consider the student's developmental level as well as special interests when choosing indicators (e.g., student can match pictures of favorite comic book characters, each one designating a different task on his work system; for another student, numbers or words may be more appropriate).

- Using the blank rectangles in the template, make one set of indicators to represent the activities/tasks/jobs to be completed. Make a matching set if the work system will be set up so that the student is to match indicators to the activity or an item related to the task.

- Select a left-to-right or top-to-bottom orientation of the work system (see Figures 86 and 87). It is a good idea to try one orientation and then the other, collecting data to determine which orientation is preferred by the student. Print the desired template on cardstock. Cut out the work system card as well as the indicators.

- Laminate all pieces, if possible.

- Place a hard piece of sticky-back Velcro® on each indicator. Place a soft piece of sticky-back Velcro® on the work system card to correspond to the number of indicators.

Templates:

Matching Work System Card – Top-to-Bottom Orientation

How much work?	Templates for Indicators	
What's next?		

Figures 86. Work system card templates – top-to-bottom orientation.

Matching Work System Card – Left-to-Right Orientation

How much work?	What's next?

Figures 87. Work system card templates – left-to-right orientation.

Checklists

. . .

Raphael has a tough time organizing his time, analyzing what needs to be done, and using his problem-solving skills to make sure that what needs to get done actually gets done. After a great deal of frustration, and many conversations regarding his household responsibilities, his parents decided to try posting a checklist of the tasks he had to complete each day. They told him that he could complete the tasks in any order but that all of them had to be checked off by the end of the day.

Raphael found the checklist easy to use and seemed to appreciate the fact that he could see what was expected each day. His parents appreciated the fact that Raphael completed his daily tasks without arguing and that he showed initiative regarding completing the tasks independently and without reminders.

. . .

A checklist can be an effective way to organize tasks so that a student with EF deficits knows *what* exactly needs to be done, *how much* work is expected to be completed, and *when* the work is done. A checklist lists the tasks that have to be completed and provides a means of checking off completed tasks. As memory tools helpful for a variety of purposes (Aspy & Grossman, 2012), checklists may be used to support students with tasks related to homework, social interaction, household chores, and personal hygiene (McClannahan & Krantz, 2010), as well as tasks and routines at school.

A checklist may be printed on a piece of paper, with a box or a line for checking off items, or it can be written on a whiteboard, where completed tasks can be easily erased. Alternately, a magnetic whiteboard can be used and a magnet can be moved from a "not finished" to a "finished" column on the whiteboard.

When implementing a checklist, begin by listing the tasks that have to be completed in a day. As the student becomes used to the checklist, you can transition to a checklist that covers more time. The family of one of the authors began with a daily checklist that included a magnet that could be moved from one side to the other (see Figure 88). They are now using a weekly checklist, printed on a whiteboard, that allows for tasks to be erased or checked off when completed (see Figure 89).

Task to Be Completed	Not Completed	Completed
Feed pets		
Empty dishwasher		
Make bed		
Take out trash		

Figure 88. Example of a daily checklist with a space for a magnet to be moved from the "Not Completed" to the "Completed" column.

Monday	Tuesday	Wednesday	Thursday	Friday	Saturday	Sunday
Take out trash	Empty dishwasher	Help with dinner	Fill dishwasher	Take out trash	Cut grass	Tidy room
Do homework	Do homework	Do homework	Do homework	Read for 20 minutes	Write to Grandma	Do laundry

Figure 89. Example of a weekly checklist with items to be crossed off when completed.

Figures 90 and 91 show additional examples of checklists.

Danny's Jobs for _____

☐ Take out the trash

☐ Load the dishwasher

☐ Walk the dog

☐ Read for 20 minutes

Checklist with distinct tasks

Figure 90. Checklist with distinct tasks listed and a box for checking off completed tasks.

Loading the Dishwasher:

☐ Rinse all dishes before putting them in the dishwasher (there should be no big chunks of food)

☐ Put glasses and small bowls on the top shelf

☐ Put bigger items on the bottom shelf

☐ Put utensils in the utensil holder – knives go sharp-side down

☐ Put one dishwasher tablet in the dispenser and close it

☐ Close the door and turn the knob to "normal"

Checklist with distinct steps of a task

Figure 91. Checklist with distinct steps of a task listed and a box for checking off completed tasks.

Make a Checklist

Function:

The function of a checklist is to communicate expectations for the set of tasks or jobs a student will complete during a specified amount of time. A checklist can be made for the tasks to be completed in a day or a week, or for the steps that have to be completed to finish a more complicated task.

When/How to Use:

- Use a checklist (see template in Figure 92) any time there are several tasks to be done or there are several steps needed to complete a task. In order for a checklist to be effective, the student must be able to read the tasks on the list and understand the concept of checking off a task once it is completed. Alternately, for a student who cannot read, pictures or icons may be used in place of written words.

Templates:

Simple Checklist _____'s Jobs for _____ Name: _____ Date: _____	✔ When completed
       When you are all done, you can _____	

Figure 92. Sample template for a daily checklist.

Task Analysis

. . .

When it was time to get ready to go home at the end of the day, Celeste struggled with the routine. Many times she would leave for the bus without the necessary materials to complete her homework. When the teacher provided a transition cue to let the students know that it was time to prepare to go home, Celeste could be found observing the fish in the fish tank or talking to her classmates. It was not uncommon for her to exit the classroom without her coat, lunchbox, or even her backpack.

Though Celeste's instructional assistant would verbally remind her that she needed to prepare to leave for the day, quite often Celeste left out some of the steps in the getting-ready-to-go-home process. Her IEP team implemented a task analysis, breaking down each step in the process of getting ready to go home and teaching those steps one component at a time. Celeste now completes this routine successfully.

. . .

Do you remember learning how to compute a three-digit by three-digit multiplication problem? Think about all the steps required to complete this task. There are quite a few! It is easy to overlook the complexity of tasks that we have come to complete without too much thought.

For students who have difficulty mastering content that is presented in a traditional way, think about the task we are expecting them to accomplish. If it consists of interconnected parts, we might analyze the task or target skill to determine if it can be broken into component parts, or "links" in a behavior chain, that can be separated and successfully taught. This process is referred to as task analysis.

Task analysis involves differentiating tasks into discrete units or subordinate skills that the student can master one step at a time. When the student has demonstrated success on one task, the next step in the hierarchy is presented. As each step of the process is learned, it is added to the chain until the task can be completed independently.

Task analysis can be effectively used in academic, behavioral, communication, and social domains (Szidon & Franzone, 2010), and can be used both for simple tasks such as tying shoelaces and for more complex multiple-step procedures such as writing an essay or progressing through a complex algebraic equation. Other strategies presented in this book, such as social narratives: story format, reinforcement, and video modeling may be used to facilitate acquisition of the smaller steps (Wong et al., 2013).

Teaching the behaviors from the beginning of the chain of tasks to be completed, requiring the learner to display increasing amounts of simple behaviors at the front of the chain is called **forward chaining**. The first component of the chain is taught through prompting and fading. Once this component has been learned, the second component is added. For example, once Celeste's IEP team determined what steps were necessary for her to prepare to leave for the day, her instructional assistant taught her the first step: to copy homework in her daily planner. Once Celeste mastered that skill, the second step, taking the books out of her desk that she needed to take home, was taught. This sequence continued until all components of the chain were learned.

The opposite, **backward chaining,** may be used when the student does not perform many of the steps in the task analysis without adult assistance. In this type of chaining procedure, the last component of the chain is taught first. Once the last response in the chain occurs consistently when the last instruction is presented, the next-to-last component is taught, and this training sequence proceeds until the learner has learned all of the components in the chain. For example, in teaching a student the sequence of steps required to complete a puzzle, the student is presented with a puzzle with all but the last piece in place. Then she is presented with a puzzle with all but the last two pieces in place, etc.

· · ·

Peter's favorite snack after school was a peanut-butter-and-jelly sandwich. His parents wanted him to prepare this snack independently, but he had difficulty coordinating the sequential steps that comprise making this type of sandwich.

To help him perform this task without the assistance of an adult, his parents implemented a task analysis. When they analyzed the task, they were able to determine which "links" in the behavior chain were missing in Peter's performance (see Figure 93). They then taught and reinforced each component skill until Peter could successfully integrate all of the necessary steps. An additional strategy that was used to teach this skill included video modeling, through which Peter's sister successfully demonstrated each step in the sandwich-making sequence. Peter's parents monitored his progress, and data collected indicate that, as a result of this intervention, he is able to complete all of the component steps of this task without adult prompts.

· · ·

Making a Peanut-Butter-and-Jelly Sandwich

1. Get out knife, tablespoon, and plate, and place on counter.
2. Get jelly, peanut butter, and 2 slices of bread from refrigerator and place on counter.
3. Open peanut butter jar, insert tablespoon, and scoop out enough peanut butter to fill a tablespoon.
4. Use the knife to spread peanut butter on one slice of bread.
5. Open jelly jar, insert tablespoon, and scoop out enough jam to fill the tablespoon.
6. Use the knife to spread the jelly on the other slice of bread.
7. Put both pieces of bread together, with the peanut butter and the jelly sides touching.
8. Put sandwich on plate and cut in half.
9. Put peanut butter and jelly back in the refrigerator.
10. Load knife and spoon into the dishwasher.
11. Take the sandwich to the kitchen table and eat it.

Figure 93. Task analysis example of the steps required to make a sandwich.

. . .

Because Josiah had difficulty with the morning transition from the bus to bell work (independent activities that students in Josiah's classroom are expected to complete during the first 10 minutes of their school day), one of his IEP goals was related to making this transition successfully. Prior to this intervention, Josiah demonstrated some behaviors of concern while making his way from the bus to the classroom. When he did make it to the classroom, he was verbally prompted to complete the discrete skills that comprise the morning routine task. When the staff who support Josiah analyzed the task, they were able to determine which "links" in the behavior chain were missing, provide appropriate instruction (see Figure 94), and fade the prompts. Additional strategies that were used to teach this skill included a social narrative that incorporated Josiah's interest in Spiderman to describe the expected behaviors through text and illustration and video modeling, through which another student successfully demonstrated each step in the morning routine sequence; and reinforcement. Data collected by the educators who support Josiah indicate that, as a result of this intervention, he is able to start his day independently. As illustrated in Figure 95, data collected by educators who support Josiah indicate that, as a result of this intervention, he is able to start his day independently.

Morning Routine

1. Walk to classroom

2. Enter classroom

3. Take backpack off

4. Take out communication folder

5. Hang backpack up

6. Put communication folder in basket

7. Walk to desk

8. Sit down in chair

9. Begin bell work

Figure 94. Example of a task analysis of steps required to transition from the bus to the classroom.

Data Collection Worksheet											
Student Name: Josiah						**PROMPT KEY**					
School: Apple Valley Middle School						*I = INDEPENDENT*					
						G = GESTURAL					
Teacher: Mr. Taylor						*V = VERBAL*					
						P = PHYSICAL					
Skill: Completing morning routine independently (transition from bus to first period bell work)						*NR = NO RESPONSE*					

Individual Steps Date:	9/08	9/09	9/10	9/11	9/12	9/15	9/16	9/17	9/18	9/19	9/23
1. Walk to classroom	V	V	V	G	G	I	I	I	I	I	I
2. Enter classroom	V	V	V	V	G	G	I	I	I	I	I
3. Take backpack off	V	V	V	G	G	I	I	I	I	I	I
4. Take out communication folder	V	V	V	V	V	G	G	G	I	I	I
5. Hang backpack up	P	V	V	V	V	V	V	I	I	I	I
6. Put communication folder in basket	V	V	V	V	V	G	G	I	I	I	I
7. Walk to desk	V	V	V	V	V	V	G	G	G	I	I
8. Sit down in chair	V	V	V	G	G	G	G	G	I	I	I
9. Begin bell work	NR	V	V	V	V	V	V	V	V	I	I
10.											
11.											
12.											
13.											
14.											
15.											
16.											

Comments: When Josiah was able to complete the first step independent of adult prompting, staff worked with him on subsequent steps. He had difficulty sequencing the behaviors, so a Power Card was developed to describe the expected behaviors and video modeling was used to demonstrate the sequence. Staff reinforced Josiah for demonstrating appropriate behaviors. Not only was Josiah able to complete the transition to morning routine in his first period class independently at the end of week two, he was also able to transition independently after returning to school from a long weekend.

Figure 95. Completed task analysis data sheet for Josiah's morning routine at school.

• • •

. . .

Micah, a high school student who is well aware that in most societies handshakes are the traditional method of greeting someone – whether in social settings or in school or work environments – is always eager to make the initial gesture of shaking hands with another person to let the person know that he enjoyed meeting him or her. Unfortunately, he failed to notice that his extremely firm handshakes brought tears of pain to the other person's face.

Many students learn how to shake hands appropriately by watching and observing others, but those who support Micah found that this particular task needed to be taught directly, breaking down each step and specifically teaching each component. Through the implementation of a task analysis (see Figure 96), data collected indicate that Micah is successfully demonstrating this important social skill.

How to Shake Hands

- While facing another person, extend your right hand with fingers horizontal to the ground.
- Make the flesh of your hand that is between your thumb and your index finger meet the same flesh on the other person's hand.
- Hold hand of person firmly but not too tightly
- Shake the other person's hand in an up-and-down motion 4 or 5 times.
- Disengage from the other person's hand.

Figure 96. Task analysis of steps required to shake hands with somebody.

. . .

Implement a Task Analysis

Function:

The function of a task analysis is to teach a skill that requires several steps to be performed in a certain order. The skill is broken down into smaller, more manageable components that are taught one step at a time.

When/How to Use:

A task analysis may be used with students of all ages in all settings. It can be used to teach a variety of skills related to academic tasks, social and vocational skills, domestic activities, and expected behaviors in community settings.

Step-by-Step Instructions:

1. Identify the target skill.

2. Determine what prerequisite skills the student needs to perform the target skill.

3. Define all specific steps required for mastery of the skill.

4. Confirm that the task analysis is accurate by having someone follow the steps (e.g., a capable student or a coworker); revise if needed.

5. Assess to see which steps the student already knows.

6. Determine:

   a. Procedure for chaining (forward – teaching and reinforcing the behaviors at the beginning of the chain first – or backward – the last component of the chain is taught first)

   b. How other strategies described in this book might be used to support the teaching of each step. For example, for teaching Josiah the steps involved in completing his morning routine, another student was videotaped while successfully completing each component. The videotape was shown to Josiah as part of the teaching process. In another example, Peter's parents provided reinforcement each time he mastered a new step.

7. Teach the student one step until she displays mastery of the step.

8. As mastery of each step is documented, add it to the chain until the target skill can be completed independently.

Comments:

Use the task analysis data collection worksheet (Figure 97) to define each specific step required for the mastery of a skill and to keep data on the student's progress.

Data Collection Worksheet												
Student Name:							**PROMPT KEY**					
School:							*I = INDEPENDENT*					
							G = GESTURAL					
Teacher:							*V = VERBAL*					
							P = PHYSICAL					
Skill:							*NR = NO RESPONSE*					
Individual Steps **Date:**												
1.												
2.												
3.												
4.												
5.												
6.												
7.												
8.												
9.												
10.												
11.												
12.												
13.												
14.												
15.												
16.												
17.												
Comments:												

Figure 97. Sample task analysis data sheet.

Priming

· · ·

Nicholas reads quickly but fails to comprehend much of what he reads. He picks up isolated details but does not properly evaluate important information. Further, he has difficulty considering the point of view of another person, making it unlikely that he will understand the emotions and motivations of story characters, implications, story moral, unstated cause and effect, or the personal/cultural perspective of the author.

Nicholas has two "peer buddies," typically developing students who have been selected to help him acquire important skills in the classroom and other school environments. His teacher introduced priming as an instructional strategy to his IEP team, and the team recommended using Nicholas' peer buddies as primers for reading activities. Prior to introducing a new literature topic, the teacher provides priming materials to the peer buddies, which include print or video materials that present background information relating to the new topic. Included in the print materials is a brief outline of the material to be covered as well as a graphic organizer that helps Nicholas to identify salient information and engage in more effective depth of processing. These materials are introduced to Nicholas and reviewed with him for several days prior to the first lesson on the new topic. After several weeks of using this strategy with Nicholas, his teacher has noted an improvement in his reading comprehension skills.

· · ·

Priming is an instructional strategy that previews information or activities that are likely to be challenging for a student. Used successfully both in academic instruction and social interactions (Harrower & Dunlap, 2001), priming strategically cultivates success by addressing the memory and strategy deficits that students with EF challenges may bring to a new task. The strategy can help students understand relevant and implied information, and can also be used as a previewing strategy to familiarize students with new material, thereby decreasing frustration and anxiety and increasing competence. It is not about pre-teaching content, but about setting a student up for success through creating prior context (Gagnon, 2006). For example, priming can be used to preview upcoming events like a substitute teacher, fire drill, field trip, or schedule changes due to inclement weather, so they become more predictable (Schreibman & Whalen, 2000). It can be effectively used as a problem-solving strategy in that problems (academic, behavioral, or social) are identified in advance and the student is provided with a strategy that sets him up for success. It can be used to address many EF challenges and can be effective as a proactive strategy for students who have difficulties with problem solving.

Priming is easy to use and involves minimal time. It can occur in a variety of settings, including home and school, and can be used to prime for an entire day or a specific activity. Priming can occur at home for the following day or at school at the beginning of a student's day; it can also occur at the end of the school day for the next day's assignments and activities. It is most effective when it is built in as part of the student's routine (Myles, 2007). A team approach may be helpful, but an individual can successfully use priming. Teams may include teachers, paraprofessionals, related school staff, peers, and parents as "primers" (Hume, 2010).

The priming process typically consists of four general steps (Wilde, Koegel, & Koegel, 1992):

1. **Collaboration** – General and special education teachers, paraprofessionals, administrators, related service providers, and parents bring a tremendous amount of knowledge and skill to the task of teaching a diverse population of students. It is best practice that the educators and family members who support a student work collaboratively to determine the elements needed to implement priming as an instructional strategy.

2. **Communication** – Successful implementation of priming requires effective communication among all parties involved. The teacher needs to communicate to the primer (the individual who is doing the priming; for example, the paraprofessional, related service provider, peer, etc.) information specific to the student, including which assignments need to be primed and how priming materials can be accessed (Myles, 2007); the primer needs to communicate to the teacher information regarding the effectiveness of the priming strategy; and questions that need answering may come at any time from any parties during the implementation of priming. It is critical that an ongoing method of communication be developed to keep all parties, including parents, informed. Such methods may include communicating via notes, documentation such as a weekly or monthly calendar that displays upcoming assignments or activities, email, phone calls, and scheduled meetings.

3. **Priming** – Priming takes place in the environments and at the particular times that have been determined by the student's support team. Sample priming activities are described below. Keep in mind that priming is intended to familiarize a student with new materials or information, not to make him proficient. Combine this strategy with other practices, such as providing an opportunity for the student to make a choice of priming activities and/or where the priming session will be held, as well as providing reinforcement for appropriate behaviors.

4. **Feedback** – The primer communicates the results of a priming session to the teacher and, when appropriate, other members of the student's support team. A form may be used to collect data regarding the use of the priming activities as well as the results of the priming session on the subsequent lesson or activity (see Figure 103).

Sample Priming Activities:

Prime for reading assignments to help students understand complex literature, including ana-lyzing for implied meaning and intent using PinkMonkey (www.pinkmonkey.com). This resource offers a library of online literature summaries with free study guides, book summaries, and plot notes. SparkNotes (www.sparknotes.com) is another online resource to help learners make sense of what they are expected to learn. It offers free online study guides on various academic subjects, including literature, history, and test preparation.

Encourage students to be active thinkers when exposed to new information. This is a relentless challenge for educators and parents who support students at all grade levels. KWL, a reading/thinking strategy created by Donna Ogle (Ogle, 1986), builds on the student's prior knowledge and natural curiosity to learn more and continues to be a popular process that is useful at any grade level and in any content area. A KWL chart (see Figure 99) may be used as a priming strategy prior to the study of new material, a discussion, a reading, or an event. It requires the student to identify what is known about a particular subject or concept (K), what she wants to know (W), and what is learned as a result (L). For students who are confused about what they should be thinking when they are reading or learning new material, KWL actively engages them while providing a framework they can use to construct meaning from new material.

• • •

Billy had a highly focused interest in penguins and liked to use that interest to attempt to interact with others. His understanding of penguins was very basic, limiting him to three facts to share. This did not make for the most interesting conversations, as Billy would repeat the same three facts over and over again. When asked other questions about penguins, he would state "That's all I know."

His teacher, knowing that she could use Billy's interest in penguins to motivate him in several curricular areas, encouraged him to learn more. She used the KWL strategy (see Figure 98), tapping into his prior knowledge while building on his curiosity about the topic. Billy was excited to do his "research" on the topic, which included several visits to the library with his family to check out picture books, an Internet search, and viewing a documentary related to the topic. There were at least two positive out-comes: Billy learned a lot more about penguins, and his resulting written assignment on the topic earned him an award in the school writing contest.

• • •

KWL Chart		
Student Name: Billy		Grade: K
Topic: Penguins		Date: 01/30/14
K	**W**	**L**
Penguins are black and white	Do penguins swim?	Penguins are aquatic, flightless birds
They have feathers	Can penguins fly?	Penguins feed on krill, fish, squid, and other forms of sea life while swimming underwater
They live at Sea World	What do penguins eat?	
	Where can you find penguins?	They live almost exclusively in the southern hemisphere
	Where do penguins live?	Penguins spend half of their lives on land and half in the oceans
	How do penguins move on land?	Penguins either waddle on their feet or slide on their bellies across the snow
	Do penguins make good pets?	It is not a good idea to bring a penguin home for a pet. It probably would not thrive in a typical home environment

Figure 98. Example of a priming activity used with a student highly interested in penguins.

KWL Chart		
Student Name:		Grade:
Topic:		Date:
K – What Is **K**nown	**W** – What the Student **W**ants to Know	**L** – What Is **L**earned

Figure 99. Example of a KWL chart that can be completed independently by students.

Figures100-102 show examples of priming activities for reading, writing, and other activities.

Additional priming activities for reading include . . .

• Provide opportunity to preread material.
• Give preteaching activity with graphic organizer.
• Provide a picture, visual, or graphic organizer that represents main idea of story.
• Introduce learner to unfamiliar words before being assigned a new reading passage.

Figure 100. Sample priming activities for reading.

> *The paraprofessional and other adults who support Jaz felt that priming would be an appropriate strategy to help him participate more successfully in his reading class. They worked together to determine who would prime, when the priming would take place, and what strategies might be most effective. As a result, before new reading material is introduced, the paraprofessional "now primes the pump" for Jaz by defining new vocabulary, discussing the headings in the reading material and asking Jaz to predict what the material may be about, reviewing the questions at the end of the reading assignment, as well as looking at figures, charts, photographs, and associated captions in textbooks that may be included in the reading material. Jaz's parents also receive a list of the new words before the new reading material is introduced, and they further support the priming strategy by having discussions nightly at the dinner table related to the new vocabulary.*

Sample priming activities for writing include . . .

• Give prewriting activity using graphic organizers to help originate ideas.
• Have the student visualize what final project will look like.
• Create experiences/activities linked to the topic so that the student develops some prior knowledge.
• Use props to introduce the concepts within a topic.

Figure 101. Sample priming activities for writing.

• • •

> *Josiah recently emigrated from Germany. His Spanish class was assigned a large writing project related to Spanish-speaking cultures. His ancestry is German, and his family has long-held traditions related to that culture, so he was in for some new*

learning experiences. His teacher primed Josiah as well as other students in the class by creating experiences and activities and allowing extensive exploration time related to the topic prior to giving the writing assignment. She brought in food items, clothing, travel posters; she also showed video clips to assist students in developing prior knowledge. Finally, Josiah's parents incorporated priming activities that included a family trip to El Pueblo de Los Angeles State Historic Park, where visitors get a flavor for the architecture, clothing, and foods that were common under the city's Spanish and Mexican rule of years past. These priming strategies familiarized Josiah with new concepts, increasing his success on his writing assignment.

• • •

Additional sample priming activities . . .

• Use a video clip as a primer before student is expected to perform behavior.
• Use a social narrative as a visual tool to make expected behavior more concrete.
• Skim a test.
• View a product sample.
• Show a visual schedule.
• Remind students of out-of-classroom behavioral expectations.

Figure 102. Additional sample priming activities.

• • •

Nicole's favorite recess activity is using the swings on the playground. Once excused for recess, she runs for the swings but often has to wait because a swing is not available. Earlier in the year, waiting for a swing was a challenge for Nicole. The staff that supports her used video modeling to have her peers demonstrate appropriate "waiting for swings" behavior. As a result, when Nicole has to wait for a swing, her behavior is now more appropriate. Her teacher continues to prime her before recess, telling Nicole that there may not be any empty swings because there are multiple classes on the playground. She is reminded that she can take her place in line and that when she gets to the front of the line she can count to 100 before asking for her turn on a swing. Nicole's parents report that, as a result of the implementation of this priming strategy at school, Nicole is now also demonstrating more appropriate waiting-for-her-turn-on-the-swings behavior on her neighborhood playground.

• • •

Priming Activity Plan

Student Name:_____

Educational Settings: _____

Planning Team Members: _____

Date	Activity/ Assignment	Teacher	Primer	Priming Activities	Comments/ Feedback/ Effectiveness 1-5

Figure 103. Priming activity plan.

Metacognitive Problem Solving

. . .

Dominique had a rough weekend and refuses to go to school on Monday morning. On Friday evening her classmate, Kalen, posted a picture of herself in a new outfit on a social media site. Dominique responded to the post saying she thought the outfit was ugly and that it made Kalen look fat. Kalen responded by posting several unkind things about Dominique, including calling her stupid and ugly. Dominique was puzzled by Kalen's response because she felt she had been honest. After all, Kalen's post included the question, "What do you think of my new outfit?" Dominique was simply answering the question honestly. Throughout the weekend Kalen, along with several other girls, lambasted Dominique on social media. This resulted in Dominique becoming more and more frustrated and increasingly fixated on the problem. Dominique's mother realized she needed a strategy to help her daughter to identify solutions to the problem, allowing her to solve the problem or to let it go and move on.

. . .

Students with EF deficits may need support from adults to learn how to think differently in order to become better problem solvers. The process of learning to think proactively and metacognitively can take time and coaching.

Mataya and Owens (2013) have developed a simple, yet profound, model that is applicable to students of all ages and which is useful in teaching students how to problem-solve. Figure 104 shows the Problem-Solving Chart, which is designed to be a choice board.

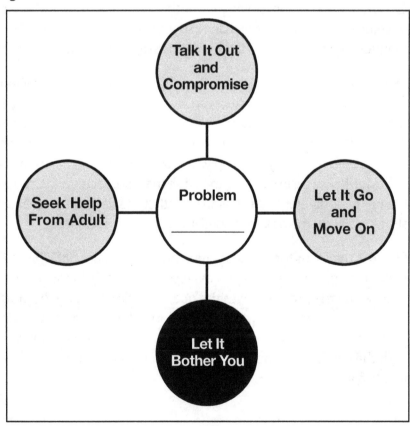

Figure 104. Basic Problem-Solving Chart. Used with permisssion.

Although the strategies are not designed to be used in a specific order, many students start at Seek Help From Adult and then rotate through the other strategies (Talk It Out and Compromise, Let It Go and Move On, and Let It Bother You) in a clockwise direction. The Problem-Solving Chart provides a visual cue that can support students in identifying a number of possible solutions to a problem, with the goal of choosing the best solution to the problem. The basic chart can be individualized to meet the needs of a specific student, and pictures and words may be used on the chart, depending on the reading level and needs of the student.

· · ·

Ivan, who is in the sixth grade, hates to go to P.E. because of the requirement to change into gym clothes in the locker room before class. One of the other boys in his P.E. class regularly laughs at Ivan and makes fun of him in the locker room.

Ivan's teacher notices that Ivan has stopped changing for P.E. and discusses the situation with him. His teacher decides to use the Problem-Solving Chart with Ivan. He makes a copy of the chart and gives it to Ivan to keep in his notebook. Using the chart, Ivan is able to identify the problem and arrive at a solution. Ivan decides that he will try to Talk It Out and Compromise, with the hope that he will be able to come to an agreement with the other boy in his class.

· · ·

Collaborative problem solving is another effective model. Massachusetts General Hospital developed Collaborative Problem Solving (CPS) to build social-emotional skills in young people manifesting behavioral difficulties (Pollastri, Epstein, Heath, & Ablon, 2013).

CPS outlines three basic plans (A, B, and C) that adults can use when a young person is not meeting the expectations of the adult(s) with whom the child is interacting. In Plan A, the adult imposes his or her will on the child. Although Plan A might result in the child complying with the expectation, it does not teach the child how to make better choices in the future. In addition, for children who lack the skills necessary to comply with adult authority, the use of Plan A may result in challenging behavior. In Plan C, in contrast, the adult makes a decision to drop a certain expectation for the time being. This is different than "giving in" in that the decision to let an expectation go for a time is made strategically, on the basis of prioritizing certain expectations.

Plan B is the focus for metacognitive problem solving (MCPS). In Plan B, the adult coaches the child through a three-step process (see Figure 105). In the first step, the adult asks the student to describe the problem, with the goal of understanding the student's viewpoint regarding the problem. The second step is an opportunity for the adult to share his concerns regarding the problem. The final step involves brainstorming possible solutions, assessing them for best fit with the concerns of the adult and the child, and ultimately identifying a solution that is mutually satisfying and realistic.

1. **Identify/understand the view or perspective of the child about the problem to be solved.**

2. **Identify/share the concerns the adult has about the problem**

3. **Brainstorm solutions together, assess possible solutions and choose a mutually satisfactory and realistic solution.**

Figure 105. Three-step problem-solving process.

Coaching Problem Solving

Function:

The function of the metacognitive problem-solving process is to support the student in understanding the views/feelings of others, generating several solutions to a problem, and selecting the best. The goal of the process is for the student to be able to independently go through the process to solve problems in the future.

When/How to Use:

- Introduce the MCPS process to the student by showing her the MCPS map and going over each prompt on the map.

- Work through each point, charting responses on a separate piece of paper or on chart paper.

- After reading Step 1, assure the student that the problem will not be solved by the imposition of the adult.

- After working through the three points, answer the follow-up question.

MCPS Map:

1. What is your perception of the problem? What are your concerns in regards to this problem?

2. My concerns regarding this problem are …

3. What are all the solutions we can think of? Which one is most realistic and answers the concerns that we both have?

Concluding reflective question:

a) How has this process been helpful in solving the problem?

Adapted from Collaborative Problem Solving, Massachusetts General Hospital. Used with permission. For more information about Collaborative Problem Solving, see www.thinkkids.org

References

American Psychiatric Association. (2013). *Diagnostic and statistical manual of mental disorders* (5th ed.). Arlington, VA: Author.

Aspy, R., & Grossman, B. G. (2012). *The Ziggurat model* (2nd ed.). Shawnee Mission, KS: AAPC Publishing.

Attwood, T. (2008, July). *Autism/Asperger Syndrome*. Presentation at the Future Horizons, Inc. Conference, Riverside, CA.

Attwood, T. (2014). An overview of autism spectrum disorders. In K. D. Buron & P. Wolfberg (Eds.), *Learners on the autism spectrum: Preparing highly qualified educators and related practitioners* (2nd ed., pp. 32-57). Shawnee Mission, KS: AAPC Publishing.

Barkley, R. A. (1997). Behavioral inhibition, sustained attention, and executive functions: Constructing a unifying theory of ADHD. *Psychological Bulletin, 121*(1), 65-94. doi:10.1037/0033-2909.121.1.65

Bellini, S. (2008). *Building social relationships: A systematic approach to teaching social interaction skills to children and adolescents with autism spectrum disorders and other social difficulties*. Shawnee Mission, KS: AAPC Publishing.

Bellini, S., & Akullian, J. (2007). A meta-analysis of video modeling and video self-modeling interventions for children and adolescents with autism spectrum disorders. *Exceptional Children, 73*(3), 264-287. Retrieved from http://search.proquest.com.library.capella.edu/docview/201148251?accountid=27965

Benton, S. B. (2001). Executive function in subtypes of children with learning disabilities. *Proquest Dissertations and Theses*, 0-1. Retrieved from http://search.proquest.com.library.capella.edu/docview/304753572?accountid=27965. (304753572).

Best, J. R., & Miller, P. H. (2010). A developmental perspective on executive function. *Child Development, 81*(6), 1641-1660. doi:10.1111/j.1467-8624.2010.01499.x

Bieber, J. (Producer). (1994). *Learning disabilities and social skills with Richard Lavoie: Last one picked ... First one picked on*. Washington, DC: Public Broadcasting Services.

Bloomfield, B. (2009, October). *Icon to I can: Visual supports for students with autism*. Presentation at the Southern California Autism Training Collaborative (SCATC) Autism Conference, Pomona, CA.

Brown. K. E., & Mirenda, P. (2011). Contingency mapping: Use of a novel visual support strategy as an adjunct to functional equivalence training. *Journal of Positive Behavior Interventions, 8*(5), 155-164.

Browning Wright, D. (2011, May). *Pacing, structuring, and transitioning for students with autism and behavior problems*. Presentation at the 32nd Annual National Institute on Legal Issues of Educating Individuals with Disabilities, Phoenix, AZ.

Burkhartsmeyer, J. (2007, May). *Cognitive characteristics of children with autism: Implications for assessment and programming*. Presentation for the Region 10 Coordinating Council, Apple Valley, CA.

Buron, K. D., & Curtis, M. (2012). *The incredible 5-point scale: Assisting students with autism spectrum disorders in understanding social interactions and controlling their emotional responses* (2nd ed.). Shawnee Mission, KS: AAPC Publishing.

Buron, K. D., & Myles, B. S. (2014). Emotional regulation. In K. D. Buron & P. Wolfberg (Eds.), *Learners on the autism spectrum: Preparing highly qualified educators and related practitioners* (2nd ed., pp. 239-263). Shawnee Mission, KS: AAPC Publishing.

Carlson, S. M., Moses, L. J., & Breton, C. (2002). How specific is the relation between executive function and theory of mind? Contributions of inhibitory control and working memory. *Infant and Child Development*. doi:10.1002/icd.298

Carnahan, C. (2008). *Structured work systems and activity organization: Online training module* (Cincinnati: University of Cincinnati, College of Education, Criminal Justice, and Human Services). In Ohio Center for Autism and Low Incidence (OCALI), *Autism internet modules*, www.autisminternetmodules.org. Columbus, OH: OCALI.

Center on the Developing Child at Harvard University. (2011). *Building the brain's "air traffic control" system: How early experiences shape the development of executive function: Working paper no. 11*. Retrieved from www.developingchild.harvard.edu

Channon, S., & Green, P. S. (1999). Executive function in depression: The role of performance strategies in aiding depressed and non-depressed participant. *Journal of Neurology, Neurosurgery, and Psychiatry, 66*(2), 162-171.

Channon, S., Pratt, P., & Robertson, M. M. (2003). Executive function, memory, and learning in Tourette's syndrome. *Neuropsychology, 17*(2), 247-254. doi:10.1037/0894-4105.17.2.247

Chasnoff, I. J. (2010). *The mystery of risk: Drugs, alcohol, pregnancy, and the vulnerable child*. Chicago, IL: NTI Upstream.

Coffin, A. B., & Smith, S. M. (2009). *The Incredible 5-point scale: Online training module* (Cincinnati: University of Cincinnati, College of Education, Criminal Justice, and Human Services). In Ohio Center for Autism and Low Incidence (OCALI), *Autism internet modules*, www.autisminternetmodules.org. Columbus, OH: OCALI.

Constable, S., Grossi, B., Moniz, A., & Ryan, L. (2013). Meeting the Common Core State Standards for students with autism. *Teaching Exceptional Children, 45*(3) 6-13.

Coyne, P., & Rood, K. (2011). Unit 3.3: Executive function and organization for youth with autism spectrum disorder. In *Preparing youth with autism spectrum disorder for adulthood*. Columbia, OR: Columbia Regional Program. Retrieved from http://impactofspecialneeds.weebly.com/uploads/3/4/1/9/3419723/aut_unit3.3_organization.pdf

References

Danielsson, H., Henry, L., Jerker, R., Rönnberg, J., & Nilsson, L-G. (2010). Executive functions in individuals with intellectual disability. *Research in Developmental Disabilities, 31*(6), 1299-1304. Retrieved from http://dx.doi.org/10.1016/j.ridd.2010.07.012

Duncan, M., Rock, M., & Szakacs, W. (2010). *Supporting successful completion of homework for individuals with ASD: Online training module.* In Ohio Center for Autism and Low Incidence (OCALI), *Autism internet modules,* www.autisminternetmodules.org. Columbus, OH: OCALI.

Elliott, S. (2007). Positive reinforcement. In *Encyclopedia of special education: A reference for the education of children, adolescents, and adults with disabilities and other exceptional individuals.* Retrieved from http://library.capella.edu/login?url=http://search.credoreference.com/content/entry/wileyse/positive_reinforcement/0

Eysenck, M. W., Derakshan, N., Santos, R., & Calvo, M. G. (2007). Anxiety and cognitive performance: Attentional control theory. *Emotion, 7*(2), 336-353. doi:10.1037/1528-3542.7.2.336

Gagnon, E. (2001). *Power Cards: Using special interests to motivate children and youth with Asperger Syndrome and autism.* Shawnee Mission, KS: AAPC Publishing.

Gagnon, E. (2006, January). *Autism and Asperger Syndrome: Classroom strategies that really make a difference! (Grades K-12).* Presentation at the California Elementary Education Association, Ontario, CA.

Ganz, J. B. (2007). Using visual script interventions to address communication skills. *Teaching Exceptional Children, 40*(2), 54.

Green, C. R., Mihic, A. M., Nikkel, S. M., Stade, B. C., Rasmussen, C. C., Munoz, D. P., & Reynolds, J. N. (2009). Executive function deficits in children with fetal alcohol spectrum disorders (FASD) measured using the Cambridge Neuropsychological Tests Automated Battery (CANTAB). *Journal of Child Psychology & Psychiatry, 50*(6), 688-697. doi:10.1111/j.1469-7610.2008.01990.x

Harrower, J., & Dunlap, G. (2001). Including children with autism in general education classrooms: A review of effective strategies. *Behavior Modification, 25,* 762-785.

Henry, S., & Myles, B. S. (2013). *The comprehensive autism planning system (CAPS) for individuals with Asperger syndrome, autism, and related disabilities: Integrating best practices throughout the student's day* (2nd ed.). Shawnee Mission, KS: AAPC Publishing.

Hitchcock, C. H., Dowrick, P. W., & Prater, M. A. (2003). Video self-modeling intervention in school-based settings: A review. *Remedial and Special Education, 24,* 36-45, 56.

Hoff, A., & Kremen, W. (2003). Neuropsychology in schizophrenia: An update in current opinion. *Current Opinion in Psychiatry, 16*(2), 149-155.

Horner, R., & Spaulding, S. (in press). *Rewards. Psychology of classroom learning: An encyclopedia.* London, UK: Thomson.

Hume, K. (2010). Effective instructional strategies for students with autism spectrum disorders: Keys to enhancing literacy instruction. In C. Carnahan & P. Williamson (Eds.), *Quality literacy instruction for students with autism spectrum disorders* (pp. 45-84). Shawnee Mission, KS: AAPC Publishing.

Hume, K., & Odom, S. (2007). Effects of an individual work system on the independent functioning of students with autism. *Journal of Autism and Developmental Disorders, 37*(6), 1166-1180.

Jaime, K., & Knowlton, E. (2007, May). Visual supports for students with behavior and cognitive challenges. *Intervention in School and Clinic, 42*(5), 259-270.

Klin, A. (2004, May). *Understanding circumscribed interests in autism spectrum disorders.* Presentation at the 25th Annual TEACCH Conference, Chapel Hill, NC.

Kluth, P. (2010). *"You're going to love this kid!" Teaching students with autism in the inclusive classroom* (2nd ed.). Baltimore, MD: Paul H. Brookes Publishing Company.

Kluth, P., & Schwarz, P. (2008). *Just give him the whale.* Baltimore, MD: Paul H. Brookes Publishing Company.

LaCava, P. (2008). *Video modeling: An online training module* (Kansas City: University of Kansas, Special Education Department). In Ohio Center for Autism and Low Incidence (OCALI), *Autism internet modules,* www.autisminternetmodules.org. Columbus, OH: OCALI.

MacSuga, A. S., & Simonsen, B. (2011, Winter). Increasing teachers' use of evidence-based classroom management strategies through consultation: Overview and case studies. *Beyond Behavior,* 4-12.

Mataya, K., & Owens, P. (2013). *Successful problem solving for high functioning students with autism spectrum disorders.* Shawnee Mission, KS: AAPC Publishing.

McClannahan, L., & Krantz, P. (2010). *Activity schedules for children with autism: Teaching independent behavior* (2nd ed.). Bethesda, MD: Woodbine House, Inc.

McDonald, S., Gowland, A., Randall, R., Fisher, A., Osborne-Crowley, K., & Honan, C. (2014). Cognitive factors underpinning poor expressive communication skills after traumatic brain injury: Theory of mind or executive function? *Neuropsychology.* doi:10.1037/neu0000089

Mesibov, G. B., & Shea, V. (2014). Structured and environmental supports. In K. D. Buron & P. Wolfberg (Eds.), *Learners on the autism spectrum: Preparing highly qualified educators and related practitioners* (2nd ed., pp. 264-287). Shawnee Mission, KS: AAPC Publishing.

Mesibov, G. B., Shea, V., & Schopler, E. (2005). *The TEACCH approach to autism spectrum disorders.* New York, NY: Plenum Press.

Minahan, J. (2013, January 1). Responsive classroom. In *Teaching students how to wait.* Retrieved from https://www.responsiveclassroom.org/blog/teaching-students-how-wait

Myles, B. S. (2007, December 10). Priming (Reality 101: CEC's blog for new special education teachers). Retrieved from http://www.cecreality101.org/2007/12/priming.html

Myles, B. S., Trautman, M. L., & Schelvan, R. L. (2013). *The hidden curriculum for understanding unstated rules in social situations for adolescents and young adults.* Shawnee Mission, KS: AAPC Publishing.

Myles, H. M., & Kolar, A. (2013). *The hidden curriculum and other everyday challenges for elementary-age children with high-functioning autism.* Shawnee Mission, KS: AAPC Publishing.

National Education Association. (2006). *The puzzle of autism.* Washington, DC: Author.

References

Neitzel, J. (2010). *Antecedent-based interventions for children and youth with autism spectrum disorders: Online training module* (Chapel Hill, NC: National Professional Development Center on Autism Spectrum Disorders, FPG Child Development Institute, UNC-Chapel Hill). In Ohio Center for Autism and Low Incidence (OCALI). *Autism internet modules,* www.autisminternetmodules.org. Columbus, OH: OCALI.

Neitzel, J. (2010). *Reinforcement for children and youth with autism spectrum disorders: Online training module* (Chapel Hill, NC: National Professional Development Center on Autism Spectrum Disorders, FPG Child Development Institute, UNC-Chapel Hill). In Ohio Center for Autism and Low Incidence (OCALI), *Autism internet modules,* www.autisminternetmodules.org. Columbus, OH: OCALI.

Odom, S., Boyd, B. A., Hall, L. J., & Hume, K. (2010). Evaluation and treatment of comprehensive treatment models for individuals with autism spectrum disorders. *Journal of Autism and Developmental Disorders, 40*(4) 425-436.

Ogle, D. (1986). K-W-L: A teaching model that develops active reading of expository text. *The Reading Teacher,* 564-570.

Palmer, S., & Wehmeyer, M. (2003). Promoting self-determination in early elementary school. *Remedial and Special Education, 24*(2), 115-126.

Pollastri, A. R., Epstein, L. D., Heath, G. H., & Ablon, J. S. (2013). The collaborative problem solving approach: Outcomes across settings. *Harvard Review of Psychiatry, 21*(4), 188-199. Retrieved from http://www.thinkkids.org/wp-content/uploads/2013/01/CPS-Outcomes-7-2013.pdf

Schreibman. L., & Whalen, C. (2000). The use of video priming to reduce disruptive transition behavior in children with autism. *Journal of Positive Behavior Intervention, 2,* 3-12.

Siegel, B. (2003). *Helping children with autism learn: Treatment approaches for parents and professionals.* New York, NY: Oxford University Press.

Simonsen, B., Fairbanks, S., Briesch, A., Myers, D., & Sugai, G. (2008). Evidence-based practices in classroom management: Considerations for research to practice. *Education and Treatment of Children, 31,* 351-380.

Smith, S.M. (2008). *Visual supports: Online training module* (Columbus: Ohio Center for Autism and Low Incidence). In Ohio Center for Autism and Low Incidence (OCALI), *Autism internet modules,* www.autisminternetmodules.org. Columbus, Ohio: OCALI.

Sprague, J. R., & Horner, R. H. (1999). Low-frequency high-intensity problem behavior: Toward an applied technology of functional assessment and intervention. In A. C. Repp & R. H. Horner (Eds.), *Functional analysis of problem behavior: From effective assessment to effective support* (pp. 98-116). Belmont, CA: Wadsworth.

Szidon, K., & Franzone, E. (2010). *Task analysis: Online training module* (Madison, WI: National Professional Development Center on Autism Spectrum Disorders, Waisman Center, University of Wisconsin). In Ohio Center for Autism and Low Incidence (OCALI), *Autism internet modules,* www.autisminternetmodules.org. Columbus, OH: OCALI.

Vermeulen, P. (2012). *Autism as context blindness.* Shawnee Mission, KS: AAPC Publishing.

Volden, J., & Johnston, J. (1999). Cognitive scripts in autistic children and adolescents. *Journal of Autism and Developmental Disorders, 29*(3), 203-211.

Ward, S. (2013, June). *Fill my toolbox! Just treatment tools to develop executive function skills.* Presentation at Social Thinking Providers Conference, San Francisco, CA.

Watkins, L. H., Sahakian, B. J., Robertson, M. M., Veale, D. M., Rogers, R. D., Pickard, K. M., Aitken, M., & Trevor, W. (2005). Executive function in Tourette's syndrome and obsessive-compulsive disorder. *Psychological Medicine, 35*(4), 571-82. Retrieved from http://search.proquest.com.library.capella.edu/docview/204507298?accountid=27965

Wilde, L., Koegel, L., & Koegel, R. (1992). *Increasing success in school through priming: A training manual.* Santa Barbara, CA: University of California.

Wilson, D. E. (2014). *Focus moves: Integrated activities for collaboration.* Shasta, CA: Integrated Learner Press.

Winner, M. G. (2000). *Inside out: What makes a person with social cognitive deficits tick?* San Jose, CA: Author.

Winner, M. G. (2008). *Homework and beyond! Teaching organizational skills to individuals with ASD.* Retrieved from http://www.socialthinking.com/what-is-social-thinking/published-articles/102-homework-and-beyond

Winter-Messiers, M. A. (2014). Harnessing the power of special interest areas in the classroom. In K. D. Buron & P. Wolfberg (Eds.), *Learners on the autism spectrum: Preparing highly qualified educators and related practitioners* (2nd ed., pp. 288-313). Shawnee Mission, KS: AAPC Publishing.

Wong, C., Odom, S. L., Hume, K., Cox, A.W., Fettig, A., Kucharczyk, S., . . . Schultz, T. R. (2013). *Evidence-based practices for children youth, and young adults with Autism Spectrum Disorder.* Chapel Hill, NC: The University of North Carolina, Frank Porter Graham Child Development Institute, Autism-Based Practice Review Group.

Wragge, A. (2011). *Social narratives: Online training module* (Columbus, OH: OCALI). In Ohio Center for Autism and Low Incidence (OCALI), *Autism internet modules,* www.autisminternetmodules.org. Columbus, OH: OCALI.

Ybarra, O., & Winkielman, P. (2012). On-line social interactions and executive functions. *Frontiers in Human Neuroscience, 6,* 1-6.

Related Materials

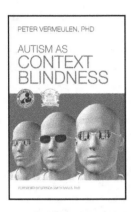

Autism as Context Blindness

by Peter Vermeulen, PhD

Full of real-life examples and often humorous, this book examines context as it relates to observation, social interactions, communication and knowledge. The author explains in everyday terms how the autistic brain functions, with a particular emphasis on the apparent lack of sensitivity to and awareness of the context in which things happen. A large part of the book focuses on how to reduce context blindness in various areas and how vital this can be for successful functioning. Due to the far-reaching consequences of context blindness, this book is a must for those living and working with somebody with ASD.

ISBN 9781937473006 | Code 9076 | Price: $34.95

STUCK! STRATEGIES

What to Do When Students Get STUCK: How to Turn "No!" Into "Let's Go!"

by Janice Carroll and Terry Ellis Izraelevitz

Children with autism spectrum and related disorders tend to literally get stuck in response to various tasks and challenges. This collection of true-and-tried strategies for home, school, and community are designed to get students "unstuck" and, therefore, ready to learn and function successfully by turning "no" into "let's go." Learn to recognize the signs early and proactively intervene in a positive manner. Consistent use of STUCK Strategies to help students get unstuck on a daily basis results in happier and better adjusted students who continue to grow. We all get stuck sometimes, and here are some bulletproof suggestions to help your STUCK! students get "unstuck."

ISBN 9781937473990 | Code 9115 | Price: $21.95

Big Picture Thinking:

Using Central Coherence Theory to Support Social Skills – A Book for Students

by Aileen Zeitz Collucci, MA, CCC

This interactive book, designed to be completed by a student or adult with social challenges, along with a support person, focuses on breaking down skills or behaviors and then putting them back together again into a manageable whole, as a way to efficiently process social situations, leading to more effective social skills. Many people who have difficulties with social cognition, including those on the autism spectrum, are not able to see the "big picture" of a situation. That is, they tend to focus, or even "hyper-focus," on the details within the larger whole of a concept, conversation, story, picture or situation, and have difficulty recognizing the main idea, topic or general point. *Big Picture Thinking* was written to help students with cognitive deficits "see" how individual pieces of social information fit into a larger context, so that they may begin to become "big picture thinkers" and, therefore, be more successful.

ISBN 9781934575864 | Code 9071 | Price: $24.95

From AAPC

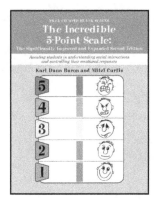

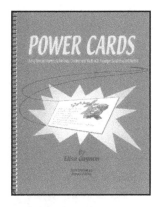

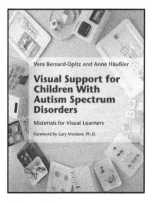

The Incredible 5-Point Scale:

The Significantly Improved and Expanded Second Edition; Assisting students in understanding social interactions and controlling their emotional responses

by Kari Dunn Buron and Mitzi Curtis

Using the same practical and user-friendly format as the first edition, Buron and Curtis let readers benefit from work done with the scales over the past 10 years, now considered "classics" in homes and classrooms across the country and abroad. Includes new scales specifically designed for young children and those with more classic presentations of autism, including expanded use of the Anxiety Curve. Another welcome addition is a list of goals and objectives related to incorporating scales in students' IEPs. Also, free materials include blank scales, small portable scales and worksheets for easy duplication. As in their other writings, the authors emphasize the importance self-management and self-regulation, two evidence-based practices.

ISBN 9781937473075 | Code 9936A | Price: $19.95

Power Cards

Using Special Interests to Motivate Children and Youth With Asperger Syndrome and Autism

by Elisa Gagnon

This step-by-step book shows parents and educators how to help change an unwanted or inappropriate behavior by capitalizing on the special interests that characterize children and youth with Asperger Syndrome. This simple approach is easy to use and makes it easier for children to learn desired behaviors. A brief, motivational text related to the child's special interest or a highly admired person is combined with an illustration, which is then made into a bookmark or business card-sized "Power Card" that the child can refer to whenever needed. For younger children, the special interest or hero is incorporated into a short story.

ISBN 9781931282017 | Code 9910 | Price: $21.95

Visual Support for Children With Autism Spectrum Disorders

Materials for Visual Learners

by Vera Bernard-Opitz, PhD, and Anne Häußler, PhD

With hundreds of colorful illustrations and step-by-step directions, this book lays the foundation for how to structure teaching environments, as well as offers countless examples of activities for students, ranging from basic skills, to reading and math, to social behavior. The authors have combined their years of experience working with individuals on the autism spectrum to bring teachers and other professionals practical ideas and teaching methods for offering visual supports to students with ASD and other visual learners.

ISBN 9781934575826 | Code 9065 | Price: $34.95

To order, please visit www.aapcpublishing.net

P.O. Box 23173
Shawnee Mission, Kansas 66283-0173
www.aapcpublishing.net

CPSIA information can be obtained
at www.ICGtesting.com
Printed in the USA
BVHW060008190521
607638BV00009B/1086